BORDER COLLIES
KW-192

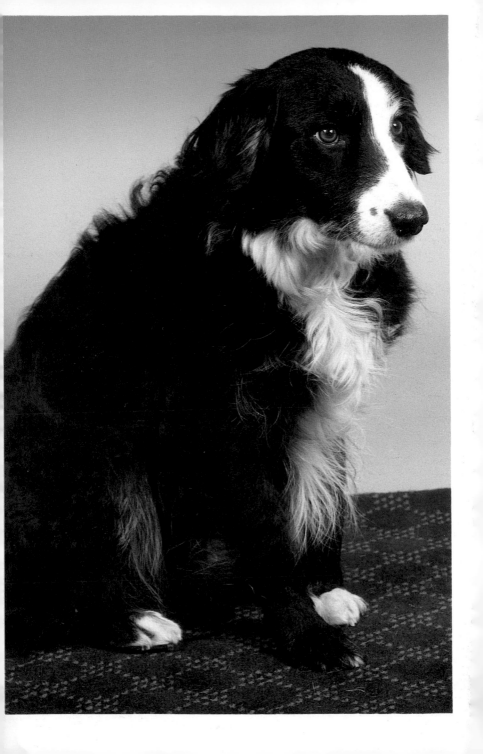

As a home companion, the Border Collie is a biddable and obedient dog, with no small amount of loyalty for its master. Owner, Vivian Bregman.

Contents

Title page: *Its intelligence, eagerness, and no-nonsense work ethic have earned the Border Collie a popular position as a pet and working dog in England and the United States. Border Collie owned by Ken Sigel.*

Photography: Isabelle Francais, Ron Moat, Vince Serbin, and Sally Anne Thompson.

Drawings: Scott Boldt, Richard Crammer, Richard Davis, Andrew Prendimano, John Quinn, and Alexandra Suchenka.

The text of this book is the result of the joint effort of the authors and the editorial staff of T.F.H. Publications, Inc., which is the originator of all sections of the book except the chapters entitled "History of the Border Collie," "The Versatility of the Border Collie," "Sheep Dog Trials," "The Border in America," and "Australia and the Border." Additionally, the portrayal of canine pet products in this book is for general instructive value only; the appearance of such products does not necessarily constitute an endorsement by the author, the publisher, or the owners of the dogs portrayed in this book.

Distributed in the UNITED STATES by T.F.H. Publications, Inc., One T.F.H. Plaza, Neptune City, NJ 07753; in CANADA to the Pet Trade by H & L Pet Supplies Inc., 27 Kingston Crescent, Kitchener, Ontario N2B 2T6; Rolf C. Hagen Ltd., 3225 Sartelon Street, Montreal 382 Quebec; in CANADA to the Book Trade by Macmillan of Canada (A Division of Canada Publishing Corporation), 164 Commander Boulevard, Agincourt, Ontario M1S 3C7; in ENGLAND by T.F.H. Publications, PO Box 15, Waterlooville PO7 6BQ; in AUSTRALIA AND THE SOUTH PACIFIC by T.F.H. (Australia) Pty. Ltd., Box 149, Brookvale 2100 N.S.W., Australia; in NEW ZEALAND by Ross Haines & Son, Ltd., 82 D Elizabeth Knox Place, Panmure, Auckland, New Zealand; in the PHILIPPINES by Bio-Research, 5 Lippay Street, San Lorenzo Village, Makati, Rizal; in SOUTH AFRICA by Multipet Pty. Ltd., P.O. Box 35347, Northway, 4065, South Africa. Published by T.F.H. Publications, Inc. Manufactured in the United States of America by T.F.H. Publications, Inc.

BORDER COLLIES

MARGARET COLLIER

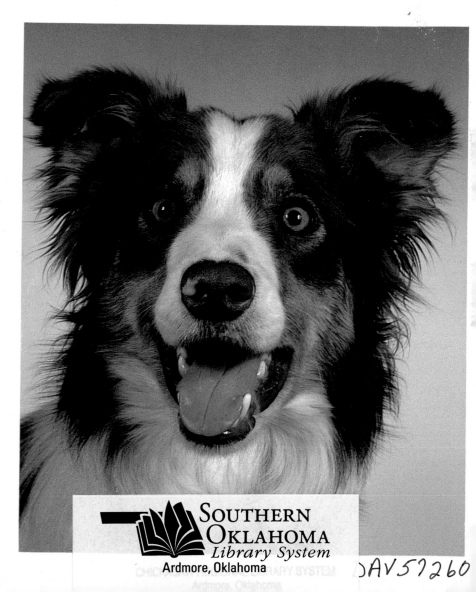

History of the Border Collie

Dogs have been part of man's life since before history was recorded. Man started to make use of them very early in their relationship. Firstly, they were used as guards for the home, and later as guards for other properties such as livestock. In early times, they were guards only, and there is no written record of dogs working with livestock in any way until the Book of Job, in the Old Testament; even here, they are but briefly referred to, and it would seem that they were guards only, even then.

The first modern reference of a dog working sheep in a similar manner to modern Border Collies is made in 1570 by Caius in his *Treatise of Englishe Dogges.*

The name "collie" was not used, though; in fact, the first mention of the word "collie" does not occur until 1617, when the habits of a Scottish bishop, who was inclined to visit on the chance of being invited for a meal, were likened to those of a "collie dog." There are several theories about the name of collie; some say it comes from the word *coley* meaning black; some say it is from the Welsh *coelius* meaning faithful, and some say it is from *colley,* which was a Scottish type of sheep. The name remains shrouded in mystery, but it seems more than likely that the designation

"Border" comes from the places where sheep dogs were mostly used, that is, on the Welsh and Scottish borders with England.

Indeed, it is difficult to know how man ever managed large flocks of sheep on the rough and hilly terrain of these areas without the help of these wonderful dogs. The strains which proved most adept at the specialized type of work required were highly prized and selectively bred from. This produced the sort of collie we know today, and from looking at very old photographs, it is remarkable how little they have changed in the last hundred years or so. It proves that the early flockmasters knew well the type of dog that was built on the correct lines for the job it was intended to do.

When the British countryside was a trifle less civilized than it is today, a certain amount of sheep-rustling was carried out, particularly in the Border regions of Scotland and England. The rustlers were called "reivers" and, of course, a sheep dog was

Facing page: *With an alert expression and an unmistakably agreeable disposition, this old British sheep dog proceeds to herd new dog lovers into its corral. Owner, Janice Demello.*

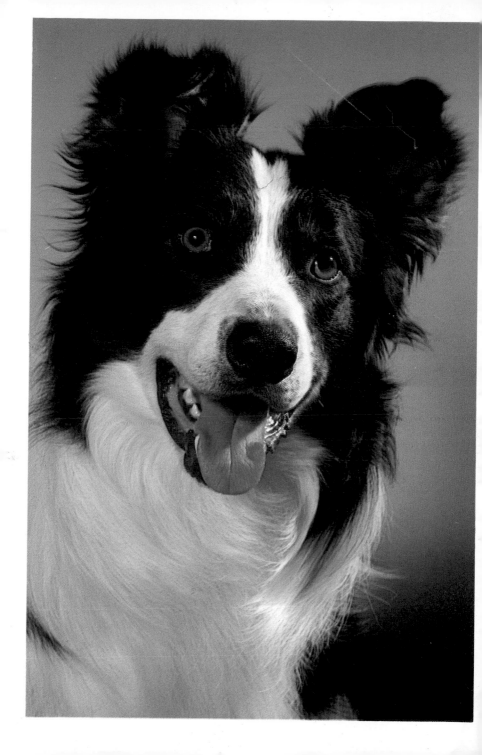

a very useful asset on these outings. The Border Collie is noted for its silent method of working, and it would seem likely that the markings which appear on so many of today's dogs were a great help, as they broke up the outline of the dog in the dark and made it less obvious to anyone who might be around. Fortunately, things are now much more civilized, and although there are still many Border Collies in the Border area, they are doing an honest day's work with the sheep.

In Bewick's *History of Quadrupeds,* published in 1790, there is a woodcut of the shepherd's dog. It bears a strong resemblance to the modern Border Collie and, indeed, to the dogs that have appeared in pictures over the last two hundred years or so. The dog was, obviously, physically as near perfect for the job as possible at that early stage of its development, so the owners of the modern Border Collie are very privileged to own such a marvelous breed.

Men were justifiably proud of their wonderful dogs, and many are the tales of the tremendous wisdom and courage shown by the dogs. In 1873 the first sheep dog trial was held to test the working ability of the dogs. A course was devised, and the sheep had to be guided around it by the dog. The dogs were given the same number of sheep to work, and every effort was made to make the run the same for each dog. The judges then scored each dog and a winner was determined. Quite often a "type" competition was held in conjunction with the trial, and it was surprising how often the best working dog was also the best looking. The winning dogs became very desirable, and it wasn't long before people started to think about keeping a registry of them. The winning dogs were fetching very high prices when sold, the almost hypnotic "eye" then considered totally unique to the Border Collie; it was the best sort of sheep dog to have. In 1906 the International Sheep Dog Society was formed and written records instituted. Now that the dogs had the "shop window" of trials and a society to prove the breeding, they became sought-after all over the world. Even at that time, it was not unusual for a dog to be sold in Australia or New Zealand for a four-figure sum. Indeed, several of the dogs that won the Society's supreme

While the Border makes ample use of its strong "eye," a determined bark helps to convince the more stubborn of the flock. Owner, John Weikel.

championship became the forerunners of the breed in Australia and New Zealand. Some well-known trainers of the day were able to sell working dogs abroad for a very good price and make a very good living. British dogs are still in demand overseas. Today the U.S.A. is quite a large importer, and some Borders go to Continental Europe. After the Falklands War, at least one consignment of puppies went out to the Islands to help re-stock the sheep-dog population. Without this marvelous and untiring work force, it is unlikely that countries who depend heavily on sheep could cope.

The first stud books (kept since 1906) put out by the International Sheep Dog Society averaged about 1000 dogs per issue; now there are at least 7000 per year, and this does not cover all the dogs which are recorded by societies in their own countries. These days, there is an increasing number of Border Collies not registered with a sheep dog society, but instead with the kennel club of their respective countries.

For about 50 years, the Border Collie has been recognized as a show dog in both Australia and New Zealand; naturally, they have developed a "show" type. Hopefully, the dog is still capable, both physically and mentally, of doing the job for

History of the Border Collie

Working with owner-handler Mrs. Sarah Davies, this handsome collie is "Mist," sponsored by the Nylabone Corporation of Great Britain to compete in an obedience event.

which it was bred. Indeed, there are reports of dogs in these countries taking on a working role after they have proved themselves in the show ring.

On the Continent too, the Border Collie has been recognized for the breed ring for much longer than it has in Britain, its country of origin. In Britain, the breed did not enter the show ring until 1976, when it received Kennel Club recognition. They had been accepted on the obedience and working trials register for many years, and had already proved themselves the top dog in all such pursuits. Now they have the chance to prove that they are as good-looking as they are intelligent.

In the U.K., to ensure that the show Border Collie will not lose his working ability, before he can gain the title of champion he must take a working test to prove he can do the job for which he was originally bred. If he cannot, he must be content with the title of show champion. Presently, there is no dog in the U.K. who has gained the title of champion—they are all show champions. Although some dogs would be more than capable of earning their qualification, in some cases the owners are reluctant to risk their dogs at what can be a chancy occupation. Perhaps this is understandable.

The Border Collie is, undoubtedly, the best and most popular dog in obedience and agility competitions, and in the U.S. it is very popular in Frisbee®-catching competitions. As if this weren't enough, it does very well in working trials the world over.

It has become very much more than "just" a sheep dog, and has paid a heavy price for such popularity. Many people see it as a pretty, very biddable and attractive pet, which it can be, but people seeing it on television or in competition seem to forget the long hours of training which make it so obedient and biddable.

A Border Collie from the correct source can be a charming pet, but dogs from a strong working line can become very frustrated and destructive if they find themselves in an environment where there is nothing for them to do. The job is the Border Collie's reason for living. The desperate need to work is slightly diluted in certain lines bred for the show ring, but it should be remembered that, although this marvelous dog is usually quite happy to be a loving pet, he will need plenty of exercise, and preferably some occupation for his very able brain.

In the widely acclaimed and lavishly illustrated *The Atlas of Dog Breeds of the World* (H-1091) and the larger, encyclopedic *The Canine Lexicon* (TS-175), the Border Collie as well as related breeds are discussed in insightful detail.

"Mist" relaxes after a great catch—the Nyladisc®. For an active breed like the Border Collie, exercise stimulates the mind and body of the dog.

Above: *"Mist" performs an agility event with ease and confidence.*
Below: *Borders who principally compete in dog shows perform in obedience with great competence. This accomplished Border is as handsome as he is agile.*

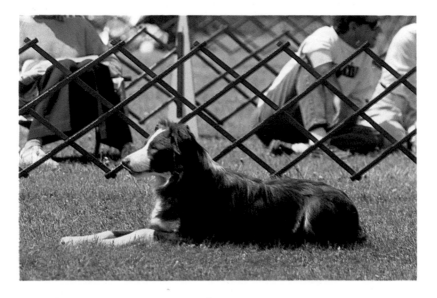

The Versatility of the Border Collie

The Border Collie is never happier than when doing something. Such is their desire to please that they are willing to be trained to do most things, and they usually excel in the field chosen for them by their owner. Although the premier sheep dog, the Border Collie is not averse to turning his paw to anything that involves work or pleasure in any sphere.

As can be seen from the list of competitors at the Crufts Obedience Championships, Border Collies and their unregistered counterparts, the working sheep dog, have made obedience their own. They are the dog to beat, at Crufts as well

Border Collie takes the long jump at an obedience competition. Notice the matter-of-fact expression on the face of this airborne and confident Border.

as the many shows held throughout the country. They relish working with their handlers, and seem to find little difficulty in adapting their sheep-

The Versatility of the Border Collie

Up and over! "Mist" lilts over the hurdle at an obedience trial. The breed's agility and interest in work make the Border Collie excel in many kinds of organized dog competition.

working habits to obedience, which, on the face of it, appears to be a totally different set of skills. If you give the matter some thought, however, many of the exercises have a rough parallel to some of the skills required by sheep dogs. The heel work in obedience does require different skills to driving sheep, as the Border Collie must follow the handler's turns and pace implicitly, whereas when he is working sheep, it is up to him to direct the flock while working at a distance from the handler. The retrieve is another test which the Border Collie would not need as a sheep dog, but the dogs seem to enjoy it greatly, and will retrieve over and over again just for pleasure. The sendaway is a stylized form of outrun, and the stay tests could be construed to be part of a sheep dog's work, as the shepherd may want the dog to remain stationary to guard the sheep. Scent could also be considered as a working skill, as the dog might have to use his nose to find lost sheep or to find where they have been buried in snow. Whatever the obedience exercise, even if it is not involved with his natural skills, the Border Collie soon masters it and becomes a very difficult dog to beat in competition.

Border Collies have become the chief participant in the sport of agility. Their natural athleticism and keenness to please have made them a very suitable subject for this sport, where the main requirements are speed and the ability to clear a variety of jumps, weave through poles, and go through tunnels. If the Border Collie has a fault in this sport, it is that it can be faster than the handler, and this can lead to errors. It is no coincidence, though, that the top agility dog has been a Border Collie since they started recording winners. Working trials are yet another canine sphere where Border Collies have become the breed to beat. These tests are graduated from C.D. or Companion Dog, which is the simplest test, to U.D. or Utility Dog, to W.D. or Working Dog, and the top stake, which is T.D., Tracking Dog. There is a higher stake called P.D. or Police Dog, but few civilians take part in this trial, as it involves man-stopping work, and most civilians' dogs are pets. Therefore, unless the dog is exceptional, the two are often not compatible. Besides which, Border Collies do not usually have either the size or the weight to stop a man in his tracks by holding on to his arm as is required in this stake.

Compared to the work of moving milling, unwilling livestock, an obedience event such as this one requires considerably less physical and mental acumen.

The Versatility of the Border Collie

Border Collies have been used as guide dogs for the blind. The dogs are very carefully selected, as they are sometimes too fast for handlers. Guide dogs also have to have a very phlegmatic temperament, as many are a little too quick and flighty for such a responsible job. However, those who once have been allocated a Border Collie are reluctant to change their breed when the time comes for a new dog.

This wonderful breed has also been trained to work as a hearing dog for the deaf, where the dog has to alert the deaf person to sounds around him.

Demonstrating one of many talents, this smart Border returns the dumbbell.

Perhaps not the ideal job for such an energetic breed, but nevertheless, the Border Collie comes to the fore as a very good dog for the job.

One other sphere where they are most successful is in Search and Rescue. In Britain's Search and Rescue Dog Association, dogs and handlers are required to go out and look for missing climbers and walkers. A lot of these people get lost in areas where sheep are grazed. Border Collies and other search dogs have to range well ahead of the handlers in order to cover the maximum amount of ground, so that all dogs, particularly Border Collies, must be tested for their trustworthiness with sheep before training starts. It does show what an adaptable breed the Border Collie is, in that it can be taught to ignore an animal that it has been specifically bred to herd. Border Collies are becoming more and more popular for this purpose, and have been used to find bodies after plane crashes and to find people buried under buildings in earthquakes.

It would seem there is little that the Border Collie cannot be trained to do. Several Borders in Britain even act as gundogs for their owners. They take pleasure in doing anything that makes them useful, and as all-rounders, they surely are the best dogs on earth.

Sheep Dog Trials

Sheep dog trials are virtually a stylized form of farm work for the Border Collie. Most dogs in the U.K. that trial do so in addition to their daily work on the farm. It is rare that a dog is kept exclusively for trials, as the Border is too useful to be kept for a special occasion. Most of the exercises that a working dog performs on the trials field are slight modifications of jobs they perform every day of their working lives, and most sheep farmers would be lost without their dogs. Most trial winners more than earn their keep when used on the daily farm work.

Following the handler's signals, a Border Collie herds the allotted number of sheep into the pen. Quick thinking and agile movement are required of the sheep dog in order to excel at such a trial. Handler, Candy McDonald.

It is wonderful to watch a sheep dog trial and see how the slightest word or whistle gets an almost instant response from the dog. At most trials in Britain, the course is virtually the same, and the rules are easily picked up by watching. The course always starts with an "outrun" which should be pear-shaped, and takes the dog out in a wide arc behind the sheep. The dog then "lifts" the sheep by creeping up behind them and moving them towards the handler. The idea is to bring them in a straight line through the "fetch" gate, with deviations causing loss of points. When they get to the handler, the idea is to drive the sheep around him, then to move them away through the "drive" gate into a "cross drive" and through a second "drive" gate before bringing them back to the handler. In the "shedding ring," where a marked sheep is separated from the others, it is then allowed to rejoin them and all the sheep are moved to a "pen" by the dog, while the handler holds the gate open. The handler closes the pen when the sheep are inside; then the trial is finished. The dog can be disqualified by "gripping" or biting a sheep, as this is considered a terrible crime in a trialing dog. There is usually a time limit for the trial which a dog must not exceed.

Every year in the U.K., the National and International Sheep Dog Trials are held. The National trials are usually held in the respective countries, and are restricted to the top dogs from England, Scotland, Wales and Ireland. The top placed 15 from English, Scottish and Welsh trials and the top twelve from Ireland go forward to the International Supreme Championship. This is the Blue Riband of Sheep Dog Trialing and a great accolade for a dog to win. In recent years only two dogs have taken this award twice.

The Border Collie proves efficient on any number of livestock animals, ranging from sheep to goats to chickens.

In conjunction with the handler, the sheep dog awaits its next command. Sheep dog trials are among the most popular and exciting of working-dog competitions in the U.K. Owner, Ken Dugan.

VARIATIONS IN SHEEP DOG TRIALS

The main variation to the trials is the "Brace" competition, where a handler works two dogs as a pair. In some trials in countries other than the U.K., other special classes are featured, often sponsored by large concerns and enhanced prize money is on offer. Needless to say, they usually attract good entries, as no shepherd is averse to earning a little more prize money. After all, it has taken him many months, if not years, to train his dog to such a pitch of perfection.

In the U.K. some handlers specialize in Brace work. When handling two dogs, different whistles or commands must be used for each dog, and the handler works one dog on each side of the sheep. It is a very serious fault if they cross any time after the lift, and great skill is required by the handler to make sure that each dog keeps to its appointed side. Quite often a dog is tempted to move over if it thinks that its partner is not doing too well, and this is where the handler's skill becomes paramount in anticipating and correcting this.

In the U.K. it is a rare farm that can manage without a collie, but

Sheep Dog Trials

The shepherd stands to get a better look at its flock. This black and white wonder on its twos belongs to Mario Pare.

devoted worker that a farmer could have.

The natural working ability in Border Collies makes them most easy to train, yet there are some dogs that have no working instinct whatever, and will never become effective sheep workers however long they are trained. It is not unusual for farmers to buy a fully or partly trained dog, as some have neither the time or ability to train the dogs themselves. It also means that they do not waste valuable time on a dog that may not turn out to be a successful worker. Many farmers find that the cost of such a dog is well worth it.

Even good trial dogs

one does occasionally see farm workers trying to fetch the sheep on motor bikes or tractors, but nothing can surpass the Border Collie on difficult terrain, and he is very unlikely to run out of petrol. He is the most willing and

sometimes change ownership,
but the prices are very high, and
some dogs do not work well for
their new owners. Other times
they work even better, but it is
often a traumatic change for
them after they have tuned-in so
well to the original handler.

Trials are a wonderful
spectacle and a great showcase
for the Border Collie. Television
has brought them to a very wide
audience, and this has meant an
increase in spectators to trials.
People who wish to see these
marvelous dogs in the flesh and
learn to appreciate their
contribution to sheep farming
and agriculture cheer
enthusiastically at Border trials.

Above: *Less frequently seen than the
black and white Border is this pretty
working and show dog in red.*

Left: *The life of a working Border
Collie is not a glamorous one—
endless hours of shooing and shifting
dusty sheep make for a long, hard
day.*

The Border in America

by Richard F. Stratton

How ironic that, in so many cases, the show breeds have stolen the name from the actual performance breeds. Such is the case with the Collie, for the real Collie—that is, the Border Collie—has been but little known for many years. At the same time, the show Collie has been immortalized in books by Albert Payson Terhune and Eric Knight. Knight's book, *Lassie Come Home,* was made into a series of movies and, later, a television series. And so it is that in nearly everyone's mind the name "Collie" immediately evokes a Lassie-like image. The truth is the real collie, the one that outdoes all others in stock work, could no more win a show than Lassie could herd sheep!

One of the things that takes a little getting used to for the newcomer who has had experience with primarily show dogs is that there is no standard of appearance for the Border Collie, per se. The owners and breeders have learned by bitter experience that breeding for show tends to eliminate those most valuable traits that have been inbred for centuries.

Those few people who are pushing for membership of the breed in the American Kennel Club are in the minority. The AKC is primarily a show dog

This staring Border Collie demonstrates the strong-eye method of herding sheep. This preacher-like tactic requires that the sheep dog look directly into the eyes of the flock members in order to move them.

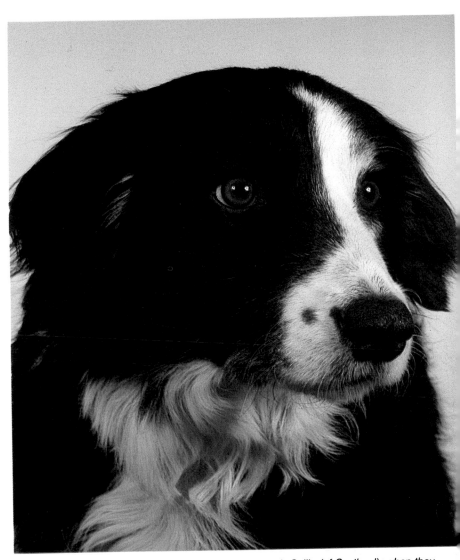

While most Americans envision "Lassie," the Rough Collie (of Scotland), when they hear the word collie, the "real collie" has always been the Border Collie. Owner, Vivian Bregman.

The Border in America

Watching a Border Collie in action often seems like a contest of wills: no matter how willful and unwilling the flock may be, the Border is always more patient and persuasive.

registry. That situation has been undergoing change in recent years, however, as the AKC has approached Border Collie people about sponsoring sheep dog trials and registering the participants in them. They have also been accepted into the Miscellaneous Class. It remains to be seen whether Border Collie people will abandon their own registries for the AKC or, at the very least, allow the AKC to take an active part in registering the breed and sponsoring its activities. At present, there is much resistance to such an alliance. After all, the Border

Collie people have gotten where they are with their own registries and field trial traditions. What possible interest is there for them to change now?

In England, the Border Collie working stock is registered with the International Sheep Dog Association, but the breed is also registered with The Kennel Club (i.e., the British show registry) and the two strains have, in effect, evolved into separate breeds: one bred for performance and one bred for show. For years the Border Collie people kept their own stud books or registered with various agricultural organizations. Don't think for one minute, though, that such a situation means the breed is not highly bred. Dr. Benson Ginsburg, Professor of Biology at the University of Chicago and a recognized authority on canine genetics, has gone on record with a statement that he regarded at least one Border Collie breeding program (the development of the Boveagh strain in Australia) as "one of the most significant projects on dog genetics and behavior" in history. And it may be of interest for the reader to know that most U.S. Border Collies are registered with the North American Sheepdog Association; for a litter to be registered with that group, an unbiased witness must certify both parents to have displayed working ability. (In

Although not all Borders are given the opportunity to excel in work and conformation, many handsome show dogs like this one fend impressively in the field.

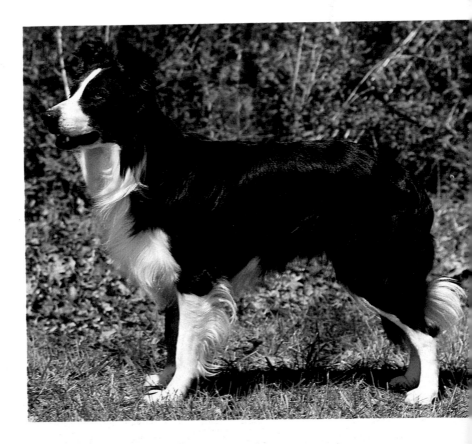

recent years, other registries, such as the North American Border Collie Association, have sprung up because of growing interest and activity in the breed, and their sheep trial results are honored by the North American Sheepdog Association. Whatever the group, it is affiliated with the International Sheepdog Association, and all the affiliates in all countries must require proof of working ability of the parents before the progeny can be registered.)

Thus, the Border Collie is bred for performance, not for looks. So, naturally, there is more variation among members of the breed than there is in show breeds, in which the individuals might as well be stamped out with cookie cutters.

Nevertheless, Border Collies are instantly recognizable, and they look the same now as they did centuries ago. Most of them are longhaired with a rough coat; however, some strains, especially many from the hotter areas of Australia, have a short coat for more efficient cooling

The long coats of these Border Collies protect the dogs from harsh winters. Short-coated dogs are preferred, however, by many British herdsmen, since despite the dog's apparent lack of insulation, the unmattable shorter coat proves advantageous.

In expression, the Border Collie is persuasively sweet and even-tempered, even comparable, many say, to the show Collie of Scotland.

and for working in rough brush. Those same dogs would be out of place, of course, in the northern latitudes of England or Scotland (not to mention the colder latitudes of the United States!).

In spite of the Border Collie's rightful place having been usurped, in the public mind at least, by the show Collie, the breed has still managed to become a film star. The making of the classic book, which Albert Payson Terhune called "the greatest dog story ever written," *Bob, Son of Battle*, into a motion picture, utilized Border Collies as the stars—even if the storyline of the book did get massacred in the manner of most books converted to film! In addition, at least two documentary-type films were made utilizing the marvelous dogs of Arthur Allen, a well-known breeder of Border Collies in the United States. More recently, a Border Collie became a star in the hit comedy *Down and Out in Beverly Hills*. This same Border Collie, along with a host of others, has been used in numerous television commercials. Border Collies are featured at state fair exhibitions, and San Diego's well-known Wild Animal Park has utilized one as a "trick dog" in its canine show. All in all, the Border Collie is becoming better known to the general public, and its charm, intelligence, grace—and yes, even its beauty—are making it ever more popular with the general populace. Such popularity is viewed with a baleful eye by the long-time aficionados of the breed. For one thing, many breeders don't want the members of their breed "wasted" as pets. With this I can't agree. After all, dogs are like rabbits—they can reproduce fast enough to supply the shepherds and stock men with their helpers. Why deprive the public of a dog that compares so favorably in intelligence, tractability, and just general good health that most other breeds pale in comparison? The justified (in my view) fear of

Although not fully recognized by the American Kennel Club, the Border Collie enjoys a sizable show-ring fancy and an enthusiastic audience. Owner, Ken Sigel.

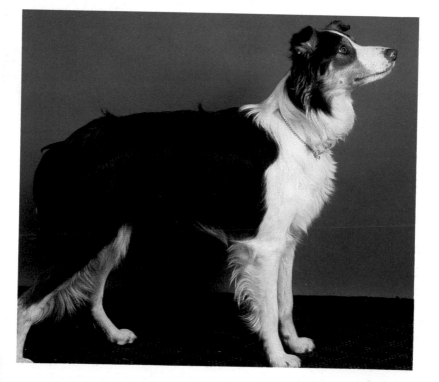

breed devotees is that the breed will become too popular, be bred by novices without regard to selectivity, and, thus, as so many breeds have, decline in quality. But knowledgeable people will avoid obtaining inferior dogs (if such a scenario develops) by only considering animals registered with the North American Sheepdog Association. Even now, only such dogs should be considered if you want to be certain of quality. Thus, there comes a rather unusual time when it is important to avoid AKC-registered animals, rather than seeking them out. (This situation may change, however, if the AKC adopts the same rules as the North American Sheepdog Association and the American Border Collie Association that allow only working stock progeny to be registered. Of the likelihood of this, most old timers are still extremely doubtful. They worry about an emphasis on show points rather than performance. Another fear is that the field trials might not be sufficiently demanding, and more status might be given to the show wins. The impetus of the AKC, after all, is as a show registry.)

Still, the siren call of these remarkable dogs is bound to be heard by the general public. They are a cinch to become extremely popular. The only question is when that will happen. Probably

Border Collie holds firmly to his Nylafloss® for clean teeth and gums. Owner, V. Bregman.

quite soon, as sheepdog trials are becoming ever more popular, with famous film stars, such as Clint Eastwood, helping to promote them. With more exposure comes more popularity as surely as night follows day. So, like it or not, the breed is becoming known and, as a concomitant of that, undeniably more popular.

Above: *This champion show dog earns his daily bread performing the true task for which it was bred.*
Below: *A plushly coated show dog from Australia, this is Champion Ebony Emerald owned by Allison J. Cowin.*

Australia and the Border

Alison J. Cowin

In Australia the Border Collie is the third most popular breed in the Working Dog Group behind the German Shepherd Dog and the Australian Cattle Dog. It has maintained this placing for a number of years, which is indicative of the breed's enormous popularity in this country.

In the early 1940s, only one or two were shown, but presently it is common to see an entry of 200 plus at breed specialties or royal agricultural shows.

The first breed standard was introduced in the 1940s, and some 50 years down the track the breed is now recognized as an Australian Working Dog, along with the Australian Cattle Dog and Australian Kelpie.

The Border Collie owes a lot of its popularity in Australia to its versatility. As a show dog it is capable of winning (and often does win) major awards at all-breeds shows and excels at obedience trialing. Many times Border Collies fill the top placings at trials and have recorded many wins at royal agricultural trials. State championships at all levels have been won by these wonderful trialers. At least five dogs and bitches have obtained their Australian Obedience Championship, the highest award for obedience and tracking.

In recent years, tracking trials have become increasingly popular, with more Border Collies obtaining their titles than ever before.

Agility trials have only just recently been introduced, and on many occasions Border Collies are filling the top positions.

Specialist clubs are running

For a working dog, a show dog, or an obedience competitor, free and unrestricted movement is strictly imperative. Demonstrating the desired gait is Australian Champion Ansauan Holly.

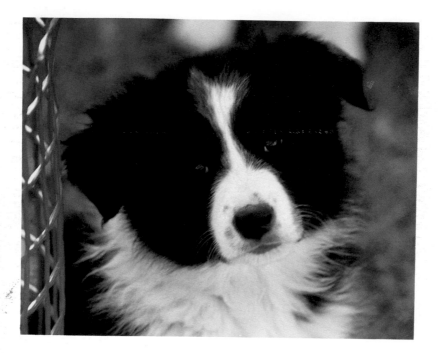

An irresistible Australian-bred Border Collie, this is future Australian Champion Bordalace Be Dazzled.

obedience and agility trials in conjunction with their breed shows and in 1990 the New South Wales Club ran a tracking trial.

Australia's sheep industry is still flourishing, and the Border Collie is an integral part of this industry. Pups for use on the land are always in demand as adults are regularly seen competing in working sheepdog trials. Needless to say, they are most successful.

It is not an uncommon practice for dogs to work during the week and compete at shows on the weekend in conformation classes. Many of these dogs have obtained their championship (bench) titles yet are still active working dogs.

All these facets—showing, obedience trialing, tracking, agility, and working—make the Border Collie a unique breed and a wonderful dog to own in Australia.

Selecting Your Dog

Now that you have decided which dog breed suits your needs, your lifestyle, and your own temperament, there will be much to consider before you make your final purchase. Buying a puppy on impulse may only cause heartbreak later on; it makes better sense to put some real thought into your canine investment, especially since it is likely that he will share many happy years with you. Which individual will you choose as your adoring companion? Ask yourself some questions as you analyze your needs and preferences for a dog, read all that you can about your particular breed, and visit as many dog shows as possible. At the shows you will be surrounded by people who can give you all the details about the breed that you are interested in buying. Decide if you want a household pet, a dog for breeding, or a show dog. Would you prefer a male or female? Puppy or adult?

Ask the seller to help you with your decision. When you have settled on the dog you want, discuss with the seller the dog's temperament, the animal's positive and negative aspects, any health problems it might have, its feeding and grooming requirements, and whether the dog has been immunized. Reputable sellers will be willing to answer any questions you might have that pertain to the dog you have selected, and often they will make themselves available if you call for advice or if you encounter problems after you've made your purchase.

This American-born red and white Border Collie was selected to serve as both companion and working dog, two of the many tasks at which the breed excels.

A bit too big?
A little **too** small.
Too fuzzy for me!
Too fat to crawl.

Before you wrap it tight
And crate it home,
Behold its appetite
And room to roam.

A sloppy yap, a barking slur,
Puppy eyes to be let free,
A him? a her? an unmarked cur,
Let's pout to see its pedigree.

The perfect pet quest:
Which pup for me is best?

ANDREW DE PRISCO

Most breeders and sellers want to see their dogs placed in loving, responsible homes; they are careful about who buys their animals. So as the dog's new owner, prepare yourself for some interrogation from the from the person who sells you your pet.

WHERE TO BUY

You can choose among several places to buy your dog. Many people think of their local pet shop as the first source for buying a puppy, and very often they're right; you should

With eyes fixed straight ahead and head held in nearly a straight line with the back, this Border Collie displays the movement of a working collie.

remember, however, that a pet shop cannot possibly stock all breeds of dog. If your pet shop does not carry the type of dog you desire, there are other places to look. One is a kennel whose business is breeding show-quality dogs; such kennels may have extra pups for sale. Another source is the one-dog owner who wants to sell the puppies from an occasional litter to pay the expenses of his small-scale breeding operation. To find such kennels and part-time breeders and hobbyists, check the classified section of your local newspaper or look in your telephone directory.

Whichever source you choose, you can usually tell in a very short time whether the puppies will make healthy and happy pets. If they are clean, plump, and lively, they are probably in good health. Sometimes you will have the advantage of seeing the puppies' dam and perhaps their sire and other relatives. Remember that the mother, having just raised a demanding family, may not be looking her best; but if she is sturdy, friendly, and well-mannered, her puppies should be too. If you feel that something is lacking in the care or condition of the dogs, it is better to look elsewhere than to buy hastily and regret it afterward. Buy a healthy dog with a good disposition, one that has been properly socialized and

Most questions regarding selection and purchase can be answered more easily after the owner determines the intentions that he has for his dog. Owner, Vivian Bregman.

likes being around people.

If you cannot find the dog you want locally, write to the secretary of the national breed club or kennel club and ask for names of breeders near you or to whom you can write for information. Puppies are sometimes shipped, sight unseen, from reputable breeders. In these instances, pictures and pedigree information are usually sent beforehand to help you decide.

Breeders can supply you with further details and helpful guidance, if you require it. Many breed clubs provide a puppy referral service, so you may want to look into this before making your final decision.

PET OR SHOW DOG

Conscientious breeders strive to maintain desirable qualities in their breed. At the same time, they are always working to improve on what they have already achieved, and they do this by referring to the breed standard of perfection. The standard describes the ideal dog, and those animals that come close to the ideal are generally selected as show

Owners of purebred dogs too often forget that all breeds of dog are interrelated. The ancient canine that is the believed ancestor of all dogs is known as Tomarctus. As packs traveled and inhabited various lands, types evolved through the process of adaptation. Later, as dogs and man joined forces, type became further diversified. This chart sketches one commonly accepted theory of the domesticated dog's development. Where does your dog fit in? With a few exceptions, dogs evolve or change as a result of a specific functional need.

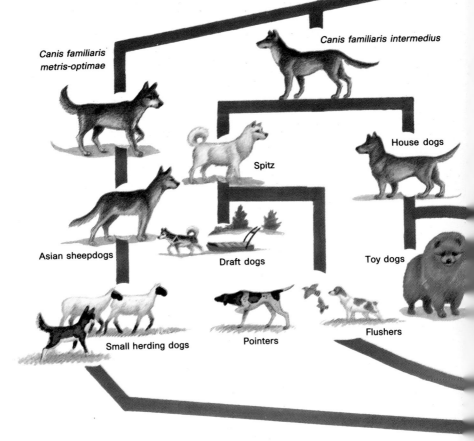

Canis familiaris intermedius

Canis familiaris metris-optimae

Spitz

House dogs

Asian sheepdogs

Draft dogs

Toy dogs

Small herding dogs

Pointers

Flushers

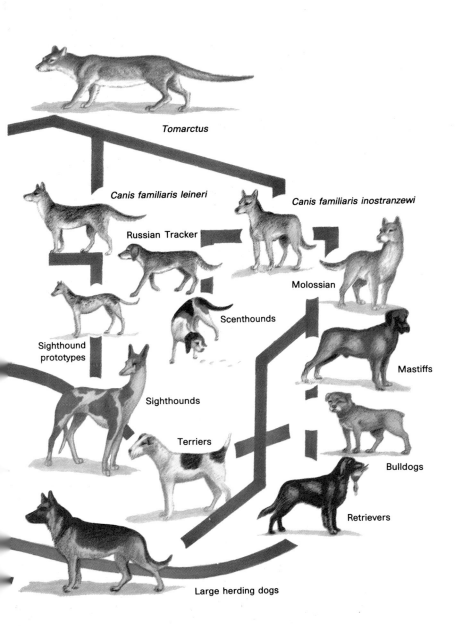

Tomarctus

Canis familiaris leineri

Canis familiaris inostranzewi

Russian Tracker

Molossian

Scenthounds

Sighthound
prototypes

Mastiffs

Sighthounds

Terriers

Bulldogs

Retrievers

Large herding dogs

stock; those that do not are culled and sold as pets. Keep in mind that pet-quality purebred dogs are in no way less healthy or attractive than show-quality specimens. Sometimes these dogs even prove more hardy. It's just that the pet may have undesirable features (such as

A variety of colors are acceptable for the breed, provided that white does not predominate. This handsome Border pup displays minimal white markings.

ears that are too large or eyes that are the wrong color for the breed) which would be faults in the show ring. Often these so-called "flaws" are detectable only by experienced breeders or show judges. Naturally the more perfect animal, in terms of its breed standard, will cost more— even though he seems almost identical to his pet-quality littermate.

If you think you may eventually want to show your dog or raise a litter of puppies, by all means buy the best you can afford. You will save expense and disappointment later on. However, if the puppy is strictly to be a pet for the children, or a companion for you, you can afford to look for a bargain. The pup that is not show material, or the older pup for which there is often less demand, or the grown dog that is not being used for breeding is occasionally available and offers opportunities to save money. Remember that your initial investment may be a bargain, but it takes good food and care— and plenty of both—to raise a healthy, vigorous puppy through to adulthood.

Facing page: *An understanding of the dog's needs is requisite knowledge for a dog owner. This handsome mate reminds us that every dog has a need to chew. Owner, Janice Demello.*

Selecting Your Dog

The price you pay for your dog is little compared to the love and devotion he will return over the many years he'll be with you. With proper care and affection, your pup should live to a ripe old age; thanks to modern veterinary science and improvements in canine nutrition, dogs today are better maintained and live longer. It is not uncommon to see dogs living well into their teens.

Generally speaking, small dogs live longer than big ones. With love and the proper care any dog will live to its optimum age. Many persons, however, opt for a particular breed because of its proven longevity. This, of course, is purely a personal decision.

MALE OR FEMALE

If you intend to breed your dog someday, by all means buy a female. You can find a suitable mate without difficulty when the time comes, and you'll have the pleasure of raising a litter of puppies. If you don't want to raise puppies, however, your female should be spayed so that she will remain a healthy, lively pet. Similarly, a male purchased as a pet, rather than as a stud

This illustration of the dog's skeleton and vital organs reveals the distinctive construction of the dog. Veterinary medicine, largely devoted to the better health of your dog, continues to make advances that promise even greater canine longevity.

According to some astrologers, dogs too are affected by their zodiac sign. If you follow the stars, be sure to select a dog born under a sky compatible with that of your birth date.

dog, should be castrated. The female is smaller than the male and generally quieter. She has less tendency to roam in search of romance, but a properly trained male can be a charming pet and has a certain difference in temperament that is appealing to many people. Male versus female is chiefly a matter of personal choice; both make fine companions.

ADULT OR PUP

Whether to buy a grown dog or a young puppy is another question. It is surely an undeniable pleasure to watch your dog grow from a lively pup to a mature, dignified dog. If you don't have the time to spend on the more frequent meals, housebreaking, and other training a puppy needs in order to become a dog you can be proud of, then choose an older, partly trained adolescent or a grown dog. If you want a show dog, remember that no one, not even an expert, can predict with one hundred percent accuracy what a puppy will be like when he grows up. The dog may seem to exhibit show potential *most* of the time, but six months is the earliest age for the would-be exhibitor to select a prospect and know that its future is in the show ring.

If you have a small child, it is best to get a puppy big enough to defend itself, one not less than four or five months old.

Older children will enjoy playing with and helping to take care of a baby pup; but at less than four months, a puppy wants to do little else but eat and sleep, and he must be protected from teasing and overtiring. You cannot expect a very young child to understand that a puppy is a fragile living being; to the youngster he is a toy like his

The Border Collie sports two coat varieties: 1) moderately long; 2) smooth. These two varieties differ only in coat appearance, with no disparity in temperament or functional ability. Border Collie owned by Annette Lenz.

"Mist" takes time out to enjoy a Nylabone®.

stuffed dog. Children, therefore, must learn how to handle and care for their young pets.

We recommend that you start with a puppy so you can raise and train it according to the rules you have established in your own home. While a dog is young, its behavior can be more easily shaped by the owner, whereas an older dog, although trainable, may be a bit set in his ways.

WHAT TO LOOK FOR IN A PUPPY

In choosing a puppy, assuming that it comes from healthy, well-bred parents, look for one that is friendly and outgoing. The biggest pup in the litter is apt to be somewhat coarse as a grown dog, while the appealing "runt of the litter" may turn out to be a timid shadow—or have a Napoleonic complex! If you want a show dog and have no experience in choosing a prospect, study the breed standard and listen carefully to the breeder on the finer points of show conformation. A breeder's prices will be in accord with his puppies' expected worth, and he will be honest with you about each pup's potential because it is to his own advantage. He wants his top-quality show puppies placed in the public eye to reflect glory on him—and to attract future buyers. Why should he sell a potential show champion to someone who just wants a pet?

Now that you have paid your money and made your choice, you are ready to depart with puppy, papers, and instructions. Make sure that you know the youngster's feeding routine, and take along some of his food. For the trip home, place him in a comfortable, sturdy carrier. Do not drive home with a puppy on your lap! If you'll be travelling for a few hours, at the very least bring along a bottle of water from the breeder and a small water dish.

PEDIGREE AND REGISTRATION

Owners of puppies are often misled by sellers with such ruses as leading the owner to believe his dog is something special. The term *pedigree papers* is quite different from the term *registration papers.* A pedigree is nothing more than a statement made by the breeder of the dog;

Dog shows are fascinating to both the participants and the spectators. If you have never attended a dog show, you are missing an important part of the canine world. This is the Crufts Show in England.

Pedigree papers can trace a dog's lineage back several generations. They do not, however, guarantee that a puppy is of good quality or sound health.

and it is written on special pedigree blanks, which are readily available from any pet shop or breed club, with the names of several generations from which the new puppy comes. It records your puppy's ancestry and other important data, such as the pup's date of birth, its breed, its sex, its sire and dam, its breeder's name and address, and so on. If your dog has had purebred champions in his background, then the pedigree papers are valuable as evidence of the good breeding behind your dog; but if the names on the pedigree paper are meaningless, then so is the paper itself. Just because a dog has a pedigree doesn't necessarily mean he is registered with a kennel club.

Registration papers from the American Kennel Club or the United Kennel Club in the United States or The Kennel Club of Great Britain attest to the fact that the mother and father of your puppy were purebred dogs of the breed represented by your puppy and that they were registered with a particular club. Normally every registered dog also has a complete pedigree available. Registration papers, which you receive when you buy a puppy, merely enable you to register your puppy. Usually the breeder has registered only the litter, so it is the new owner's responsibility to register and name an individual pup. The papers should be filled out and sent to the appropriate address printed on the application, along with the fee required for the registration. A certificate of registration will then be sent to you.

Pedigree and registration, by the way, have nothing to do with licensing, which is a local regulation applying to purebred and mongrel alike. Find out what the local ordinance is in your town or city and how it applies to your dog; then buy a license and keep it on your dog's collar for identification.

Never distracted, the Border Collie keeps to its task at hand. Years of selective breeding have helped to maintain the strict work ethic of these dogs.

The New Family Member

Whether the Border Collie in your life is a working dog, a show dog, or both, he will assuredly make a great family pet. Black and White Border Collie owned by Vivian Bregman; brown and white Border owned by Ken Sigel.

At long last, the day you have all been waiting for, your new puppy will make its grand entrance into your home. Before you bring your companion to his new residence, however, you must plan carefully for his arrival. Keep in mind that the puppy will need

The New Family Member

time to adjust to life with a different owner. He may seem a bit apprehensive about the strange surroundings in which he finds himself, having spent the first few weeks of life with his dam and littermates, but in a couple of days, with love and patience on your part, the transition will be complete.

First impressions are important, especially from the puppy's point of view, and these may very well set the pattern of his future relationship with you. You must be consistent in the

A crate, for home and travel, is standard equipment and makes an excellent gift for the new dog owner.

way you handle your pet so that he learns what is expected of him. He must come to trust and respect you as his keeper and master. Provide him with proper care and attention, and you will be rewarded with a loyal companion for many years. Considering the needs of your puppy and planning ahead will surely make the change from his former home to his new one easier.

ADVANCE PREPARATION

In preparing for your puppy's arrival, perhaps more important than anything else is to find out from the seller how the pup was maintained. What brand of food was offered and when and how often was the puppy fed? Has the pup been housebroken; if so, what method was employed? Attempt to continue whatever routine was started by the person from whom you bought your puppy; then, gradually, you can make those changes that suit you and your lifestyle. If, for example, the puppy has been paper trained, plan to stock up on newspaper. Place this newspaper toilet facility in a selected spot so that your puppy learns to use the designated area as his "bathroom." And keep on hand a supply of the dog food to which he is accustomed, as a sudden switch to new food could cause digestive upsets.

Another consideration is sleeping and resting quarters. Be sure to supply a dog bed for your pup, and introduce him to his special cozy corner so that he

A warm bed, equipped with a ticking clock, chew bone, and safe dog toy, can help a pup feel secure and welcome in its new home.

knows where to retire when he feels like taking a snooze. You'll need to buy a collar (or harness) and leash, a safe chew item (such as Nylabone® or Gumabone®), and a few grooming tools as well. A couple of sturdy feeding dishes, one for food and one for water, will be needed; and it will be necessary, beforehand, to set up a feeding station.

FINDING A VETERINARIAN
An important part of your preparations should include finding a local veterinarian who can provide quality health care in the form of routine check-ups,

The New Family Member

inoculations, and prompt medical attention in case of illness or emergency. Find out if the animal you have selected has been vaccinated against canine diseases, and make certain you secure all health certificates at the time of purchase. This information will be valuable to your veterinarian, who will want to know the puppy's complete medical history. Incidentally, don't wait until your puppy becomes sick before you seek the services of a vet; make an appointment for your pup before or soon after he takes up residence with you so that he starts out with a clean bill of health in his new home.

CHILDREN AND PUPPIES

Instruct the young members of the household on pet care. Children should learn not only to love their charges but to respect them and treat them with the consideration that one would give all living things. It must be emphasized to youngsters that the puppy has certain needs, just as humans have, and all family members must take an active role in ensuring that these needs are met. Someone must feed the puppy. Someone must walk him a couple of times a day or clean up after him if he is trained to relieve himself on newspaper. Someone must groom his coat, clean his ears, and clip his nails from time to time. Someone

must see to it that the puppy gets sufficient exercise and attention each day.

A child who has a pet to care for learns responsibility; nonetheless, parental guidance is an essential part of this learning experience. Many a child has been known to "love a pet to death," squeezing and hugging the animal in ways which are irritating or even painful. Others have been found guilty of teasing, perhaps unintentionally, and disturbing their pet while the animal is eating or resting. One must teach a child, therefore, when and how to stroke and fondle a puppy gently. In time, the child can learn how to pick up and handle the pup with care. A dog should always be supported with both hands, *not* lifted by the scruff of the neck. One hand placed under the chest, between the front legs, and the other hand supporting the dog's rear end will be comfortable and will restrain the animal as you hold and carry it. Always demonstrate to children the proper way to lift a dog.

BE A GOOD NEIGHBOR

For the sake of your dog's safety and well being, don't allow him to wander onto the property of others. Keep him confined at all times to your own yard or indoors where he won't become a nuisance. Consider what

Keen, alert, responsive and intelligent: the Border Collie possesses the mental aptitude of a working dog. Owner, Vivian Bregman.

Many dangers lurk around the house. Keep all poisonous substances and sharp objects away from your curious pup.

dangers lie ahead for an unleashed dog that has total freedom of the great outdoors, particularly when he is unsupervised by his master. There are cars and trucks to dodge on the streets and highways. There are stray animals with which to wrangle. There are poisons all around, such as car antifreeze in driveways or toxic plants and shrubs, which, if swallowed, could prove fatal. There are dognappers and sadistic people who may steal or bring harm to your beloved pet. In short, there are all sorts of nasty things waiting to hurt him. Did you know that if your dog consumes rotting garbage, there is the possibility he could go into shock or even die? And are you aware that a dog left to roam in a wooded area or field could become infected with any number of parasites if he plays with or ingests some small prey, such as a rabbit, that might be carrying these parasitic organisms? A thorn from a rosebush imbedded in the dog's foot pad, tar from a newly paved road stuck to his coat, and a wound inflicted by a wild animal all can be avoided if you take the precaution of keeping your dog in a safe enclosure where he will be protected from such dangers. Don't let your dog run loose; he is likely to stray from home and get into all sorts of trouble.

Clockwise from upper right: *pokeweed, jimson weed, foxglove, and yew. If ingested, a toxic plant can be dangerous to your dog.*

The New Family Member

GETTING ACQUAINTED

Plan to bring your new pet home in the morning so that by nightfall he will have had some time to become acquainted with you and his new environment. Avoid introducing the pup to the family around holiday time, since the extra excitement will only add to the confusion and frighten him. Let the puppy enter your home on a day when the routine

Resist the temptation to handle him too much during these first few days. And, if there are other dogs or animals around the house, make certain that all are properly introduced. If you observe fighting among the animals, or some other problem, you may have to separate all parties until they learn to accept one another. Remember that neglecting your other pets while

is normal. For those people who work during the week, a Saturday morning is an ideal time to bring the puppy to his new home. Let the puppy explore, under your watchful eye, of course, and let him come to know his new home without stress and fear.

Providing the opportunity for safe chewing exercise serves as one excellent way to provide an outlet for doggie tensions—a fact with which "Mist" will surely agree.

Facing page: *The Border Collie has a long-standing reputation for being an adaptable, highly trainable dog.*

showering the new puppy with extra attention will only cause animosity and jealousy. Make an effort to pay special attention to the other animals as well.

On that eventful first night, try not to give in and let the puppy sleep with you; otherwise, this could become a difficult habit to break. Let him cry and whimper, even if it means a night of restlessness for the entire family. Some people have had success with putting a doll or a hot water bottle wrapped in a towel in the puppy's bed as a surrogate mother, while others have placed a ticking alarm clock in the bed to simulate the heartbeat of the pup's dam and littermates. Remember that this furry little fellow is used to the warmth and security of his mother and siblings, so the adjustment to sleeping alone will take time. Select a location away from drafts and away from the feeding station for placement of his dog bed. Keep in mind, also, that the bed should be roomy enough for him to stretch out in; as he grows older, you may need to supply a larger one.

Prior to the pup's arrival, set up his room and partition it the way you would to keep an infant out of a particular area. You may want to keep his bed, his feeding station, and his toilet area all in the same room—in separate locations—or you may want to set the feeding station up in your kitchen, where meals for all family members are served. Whatever you decide, do it ahead of time so you will have that much less to worry about when your puppy finally moves in with you.

Above all else, be patient with your puppy as he adjusts to life in his new home. If you purchase a pup that is not housebroken, you will have to spend time with the dog—just as you would with a small child—until he develops proper toilet habits. Even a housebroken puppy may feel nervous in strange new surroundings and have an occasional accident. Praise and encouragement will elicit far better results than punishment or scolding. Remember that your puppy wants nothing more than to please you, thus he is anxious to learn the behavior that is required of him.

Feeding Requirements

Perhaps more than any other single aspect of your dog's development, proper feeding requires an educated and responsible dog owner. The importance of nutrition on your dog's bone and muscle growth cannot be over emphasized.

Soon after your puppy comes to live with you, he will need to be fed. Remember to ask the seller what foods were given to the youngster and stay with that diet for a while. It is important for the puppy to keep eating and to avoid skipping a meal, so entice him with the food to which he is accustomed. If you prefer to switch to some other brand of dog food, each day begin to add small quantities of the new brand to the usual food offering. Make the portions of the new food progressively larger until the pup is weaned from his former diet.

What should you feed the puppy and how often? His diet is really quite simple and relatively inexpensive to prepare. Puppies need to be fed small portions at frequent intervals, since they are growing and their activity level is high. You must ensure that your pup gains weight steadily; with an adult dog, however, growth slows down and weight must be regulated to prevent obesity and a host of other problems. At one time, it was thought that home-cooked meals were the answer, with daily rations of meat,

The canine digestive system is adapted for omnivorous eating habits. Canines require both animal and vegetable matter for good health.

vegetables, egg yolk, cereal, cheese, brewer's yeast, and vitamin supplements. With all of the nutritionally complete commercial dog food products readily available, these time-consuming preparations really are unnecessary now. A great deal of money and research has resulted in foods that we can serve our dogs with confidence and pride; and most of these commercial foods have been developed along strict guidelines according to the size, weight, and age of your dog. These products are reasonably priced,

There exists no feeding regimen that applies to all dogs. Such active individuals as "Mist" will likely require more calories on a daily basis than many less active dogs.

easy to find, and convenient to store.

THE PUPPY'S MEALS

After a puppy has been fully weaned from its mother until approximately three months of age, it needs to be fed four times a day. In the morning and evening, offer kibble (dog meal) soaked in hot water or broth, to which you have added some canned meat-based food or fresh raw meat cut into small chunks. At noon and bedtime feed him a bit of kibble or whole-grain cereal moistened with milk (moistening, by the way, makes the food easier to digest, since dogs don't typically chew their food). From three to six months, increase the portion size and offer just three meals—one milk

A dog's activity schedule must be considered when determining a feeding routine. Owner, Mario Pare.

and two meat. At six months, two meals are sufficient; at one year, a single meal can be given, supplemented with a few dry biscuits in the morning and evening. During the colder months, especially if your dog is active, you might want to mix in some wheat germ oil or corn oil or meat drippings with the meal to add extra calories. Remember to keep a bowl of cool, fresh water always on hand to help your dog regulate his body temperature and to aid in digestion.

From one year on, you may continue feeding the mature dog a single meal (in the evening, perhaps, when you have your supper), or you may prefer to divide this meal in two, offering half in the morning and the other half at night. Keep in mind that while puppies require foods in small chunks or nuggets, older dogs can handle larger pieces of food at mealtime. Discuss your dog's feeding schedule with your veterinarian; he can make suggestions about the right diet for your particular canine friend.

COMPARISON SHOPPING
With so many fine dog-food products on the market today, there is something for

Feeding Requirements

everyone's pet. You may want to serve dry food "as is" or mix it with warm water or broth. Perhaps you'll choose to combine dry food with fresh or canned preparations. Some canned foods contain all meat, but they are not complete; others are mixtures of meat and grains, which have been fortified with additional nutrients to make them more complete and balanced. There are also various packaged foods that can be served alone or as supplements and that can be left out for a few hours without spoiling. This self-feeding method, which works well for dogs that are not prone to weight problems, allows the animal to serve himself whenever he feels hungry. Many people who work during the day find these dry or semi-moist rations convenient to use, and these foods are great to bring along if you travel with your dog.

Be sure to read the labels carefully before you make your dog-food purchases. Most

Pet shops offer a large selection of quality bowls that are efficient and affordable. Offered in a wide variety of colors, bowls are easy to coordinate.

Vegetables, grains, meats and dairy products are all vital components of your dog's diet. Fortunately, commercial dog foods are nutritionally balanced and easily digestible.

reputable pet-food manufacturers list the ingredients and the nutritional content right on the can or package. Instructions are usually included so that you will know how much to feed your dog to keep him thriving and in top condition. A varied, well-balanced diet that supplies the proper amounts of protein, carbohydrate, fat, vitamins, minerals, and water is important to keep your puppy healthy and to guarantee his normal development. Adjustments to the diet can be made, under your veterinarian's supervision, according to the individual puppy, his rate of growth, his activity level, and so on. Liquid or powder vitamin and mineral supplements, or those in tablet form, are available and can be given if you need to feel certain that the diet is balanced.

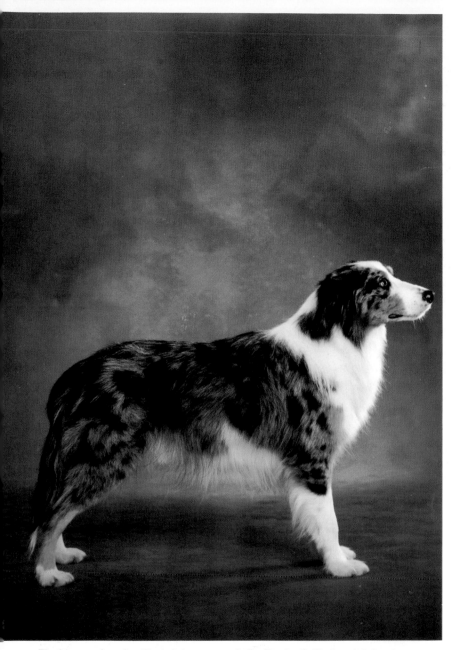

The blue merle coloration is less common in the Border Collie than it is in other herders such as the Scotch Collie and the Welsh Corgis. Nonetheless, it is an attractive coloration for this most athletic of herding dogs. Owner, Pepperland Kennels.

THE WORLD'S LARGEST SELECTION OF PET AND ANIMAL BOOKS

T.F.H. Publications publishes more than 900 books covering many hobby aspects (dogs,

. . . **BIRDS** . .

. . **CATS** . . .

. . . **ANIMALS** . . .

. . . **DOGS** . .

. . **FISH** . . .

cats, birds, fish, small animals, etc.), plus books dealing with more purely scientific aspects of the animal world (such as books about fossils, corals, sea shells, whales and octopuses). Whether you are a beginner or an advanced hobbyist you will find exactly what you're looking for among our complete listing of books. For a free catalog fill out the form on the other side of this page and mail it today. All T.F.H. books are recyclable.

Since 1952, *Tropical Fish Hobbyist* has been the source of accurate, up-to-the-minute, and fascinating information on every facet of the aquarium hobby. Join the more than 50,000 devoted readers world-wide who wouldn't miss a single issue.

DEVELOPING GOOD EATING HABITS

Try to serve your puppy his meals at the same time each day and in the same location so that he will get used to his daily routine and develop good eating habits. A bit of raw egg, cottage cheese, or table scraps (leftover food from your own meals) can

Feeding your dog need not be a messy chore, provided that non-tipping, easy-clean bowls are used for each meal.

be offered from time to time; but never accustom your dog to eating human "junk food." Cake, candy, chocolate, soda, and other snack foods are for people, not dogs. Besides, these foods provide only "empty" calories that your pet doesn't need if he is to stay healthy. Avoid offering spicy, fried, fatty, or starchy foods; rather, offer leftover meats, vegetables, and gravies. Get in the habit of feeding your puppy or your grown dog his *own* daily meals of dog food. If ever you are in doubt about what foods and how much to serve, consult your veterinarian.

Feeding Requirements

FEEDING GUIDELINES

Some things to bear in mind with regard to your dog's feeding regimen follow.

- Nutritional balance, provided by many commercial dog foods, is vital; avoid feeding a one-sided all-meat diet. Variety in the kinds of meat (beef, lamb, chicken, liver) or cereal grains (wheat, oats, corn) that you offer your dog is of secondary importance compared to the balance or "completeness" of dietary components.
- Always refrigerate opened canned food so that it doesn't spoil. Remember to remove all uneaten portions of canned or moistened food from the feeding dish as soon as the pup has finished his meal. Discard the leftover food immediately and thoroughly wash and dry the feeding dish, as a dirty dish is a breeding ground for harmful germs.
- When offering dry foods, always keep a supply of water on hand for your dog. Water should be made available at all times, even if dry foods are not left out for self-feeding. Each day the water dish should be washed with soap and hot water, rinsed well, and dried; a refill of clean, fresh water should be provided daily.
- Food and water should be served at room temperature, neither too hot nor too cold, so that it is more palatable for your puppy.
- Serve your pup's meals in sturdy hard-plastic, stainless steel, or earthenware containers, ones that won't tip over as the dog gulps his food down. Some bowls and dishes are weighted to prevent spillage, while others fit neatly into holders which offer support. Feeding dishes should be large enough to hold each meal.
- Whenever the nutritional needs of your dog change— that is to say, when it grows older or if it becomes ill, obese, or pregnant; or if it starts to nurse its young— special diets are in order. Always contact your vet for advice on these special dietary requirements.
- Feed your puppy at the same regular intervals each day; reserve treats for special occasions or, perhaps, to reward good behavior during training sessions.
- Hard foods, such as biscuits and dog meal, should be offered regularly. Chewing on these hard, dry morsels helps the dog keep its teeth clean and its gums conditioned.
- Never overfeed your dog. If given the chance, he will accept and relish every in-between-meal tidbit you offer him. This pampering will only put extra weight on your pet

Made from 89% digestible cheese protein, this Chooz™ treat is purported to be the most healthy dog chew available. If it's too hard for your dog, simply microwave it for a minute or so and it becomes a crispy, crunchy, delectable dog biscuit. It comes in many sizes.

and cause him to be unhealthy in the long run.

- Do not encourage your dog to beg for food from the table while you are eating your meals.

- Food can be effectively used by the owner to train the dog. Doggie treats are practical and often nutritional—choose your chew treats choosily.

FEEDING CHART

Age and No. of Feedings Per Day	Weight in Lbs.	Weight in Kg.	Caloric Requirement kcal M.E./Day
Puppies—Weaning to 3 months Four per day	1–3 3–6 6–12 12–20 15–30	.5–1.4 1.4–2.7 2.7–5.4 5.4–9.1 6.8–13.6	124–334 334–574 574–943 943–1384 1113–1872
Puppies—3 to 6 months Three per day	3–10 5–15 12–25 20–40 30–70	1.4–4.5 2.3–6.8 5.4–11.3 9.1–18.2 13.6–31.8	334–816 494–1113 943–1645 1384–2352 1872–3542
Puppies—6 to 12 months Two per day	6–12 12–25 20–50 40–70 70–100	2.7–5.4 5.4–11.3 9.1–22.7 18.2–31.8 31.8–45.4	574–943 943–1645 1384–2750 2352–3542 3542–4640
Normally Active Adults One or two per day	6–12 12–25 25–50 50–90 90–175	2.7–5.4 5.4–11.3 11.3–22.7 22.7–40.8 40.8–79.4	286–472 472–823 823–1375 1375–2151 2151–3675

This chart presents general parameters of a dog's caloric requirements, based on weight. The total caloric intake comes from a complete, balanced diet of quality foods. To assist owners, dog food companies generally provide the nutritional information of their product right on the label.

Accommodations

Puppies newly weaned from their mother and siblings should be kept warm at all times. As they get older, they can be acclimated gradually to cooler temperatures. When you purchase your dog, find out from the seller whether he is hardy and can withstand the rigors of outdoor living. Many breeds have been known to adapt well to a surprising number of

invest in a crate for him to call his "home" whenever he needs to be confined for short intervals. You might plan to partition off a special room, or part of a room, for your pooch; or you may find that a heated garage or finished basement works well as your dog's living quarters. If your breed can tolerate living outside, you may want to buy or build him his own dog house with an

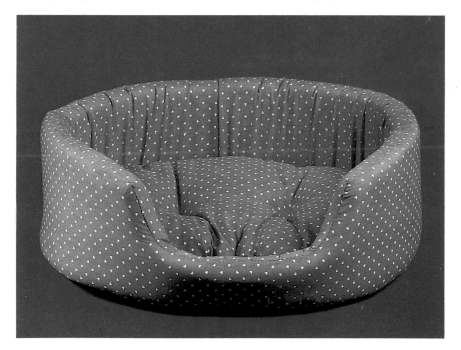

environments, so long as they are given time to adjust. If your pup is to be an indoor companion, perhaps a dog bed in the corner of the family room will suffice; or you may want to

A bed for your dog gives him a place to call his own. His bed should be placed in a warm, dry, draft-free location.

attached run. It might be feasible to place his house in your fenced-in backyard. The breed that can live outdoors fares well when given access to some sort of warm, dry shelter during periods of inclement weather. As you begin thinking about where your canine friend will spend most of his time, you'll want to consider his breed, his age, his temperament, his need for exercise, and the money, space, and resources you have available to house him.

THE DOG BED

In preparing for your puppy's arrival, it is recommended that a dog bed be waiting for him so that he has a place to sleep and rest. If you have provided him with his own bed or basket, ensure that it is placed in a warm, dry, draft-free spot that is private but at the same time near the center of family activity. Refrain from placing his bed near the feed and water dishes or his toilet area. You may want to give your puppy something with

Dog beds come in a variety of sizes and styles and are easily acquired at your local pet shop. Choose one that will accommodate your puppy when he has reached his full-grown size.

which to snuggle, such as a laundered towel or blanket or an article of old clothing. Some dogs have been known to chew apart their beds and bedding, but you can easily channel this chewing energy into more constructive behavior simply by supplying him with some safe toys or a Nylabone® pacifier for gnawing. Pet shops stock dog beds, among other supplies that you might need for your pup. Select a bed that is roomy, comfortable, and easy to clean, keeping in mind that you may have to replace the smaller bed with a larger one as the puppy grows to adulthood. Remember to clean and disinfect the bed and sleeping area from time to time, as these can become parasitic playgrounds for fleas, lice, mites, and the like.

THE CRATE

Although many dog lovers may cringe at the mere mention of the word *crate,* thinking of it as a cage or a cruel means of confinement, this handy piece of equipment can be put to good use for puppies and grown dogs alike. Even though you may love your dog to an extraordinary degree, you may not want him to have free rein of the house, particularly when you are not home to supervise him. If used properly, a crate can restrict your dog when it is not convenient to have him underfoot, *i.e.,* when guests are visiting or during your mealtimes.

A surprising number of dog owners, who originally had negative feelings about crating their dogs, have had great success using crates. The crate itself serves as a bed, provided it is furnished with bedding material, or it can be used as an indoor dog house. Not all dogs readily accept crates or being confined in them for short intervals, so for these dogs, another means of restriction must be found. But for those dogs that do adjust to spending

Crates allow for safe and easy travel and aid in the housebreaking process. Crates come in a variety of sizes, styles and colors.

time in these structures, the crate can be useful in many ways. The animal can be confined for a few hours while you are away from home or at work, or you can bring your crated dog along with you in the car when you travel or go on vacation. Crates also prove handy as carriers whenever you have to transport a sick dog to the veterinarian.

Most crates are made of sturdy wire or plastic, and some of the collapsible models can be conveniently stored or folded so that they can be moved easily from room to room or from inside the house to the yard on a warm, sunny day. If you allow your puppy or grown dog to become acquainted with its crate by cleverly propping the door open and leaving some of his favorite toys inside, in no time he will come to regard the crate as his own doggie haven. As with a dog bed, place the crate away from drafts in a dry, warm spot; refrain from placing food and water dishes in it, as these only crowd the space and offer opportunity for spillage.

If you need to confine your puppy so that he can't get into mischief while you're not home, remember to consider the animal's needs at all times. Select a large crate, one in which the dog can stand up and move around comfortably; in fact, bigger is better in this context.

The crate you choose for your dog should be appropriately sized. A crate can provide the new pet with a sense of security and belonging. Easily accessible, crates are an inexpensive, sensible investment.

Never leave the animal confined for more than a few hours at a time without letting him out to exercise, play, and, if necessary, relieve himself. Never crate a dog for ten hours, for example, unless you keep the door to the crate open so that he can get out for food and water and to stretch a bit. If long intervals of confinement are necessary, consider placing the unlatched crate in a partitioned section of your house or apartment.

Crates have become the answer for many a dog owner faced with the dilemma of either

Accommodations

getting rid of a destructive dog or living with him despite his bad habits. People who have neither the time nor the patience to train their dogs, or to modify undesirable behavior patterns, can at least restrain their pets during the times they can't be there to supervise. So long as the crate is used in a humane fashion, whereby a dog is confined for no more than a few hours at any one time, it can figure importantly in a dog owner's life. Show dogs, incidentally, learn at an early age that much time will be spent in and out of crates while they are on the show circuit. Many canine celebrities are kept in their crates until they are called to ringside, and they spend many hours crated to and from the shows.

THE DOG HOUSE

These structures, often made of wood, should be sturdy and

Consider your dog's present and fully grown size before purchasing the proper crate for him.

Commercial dog houses are designed for comfort and pest control.

offer enough room for your dog to stretch out in when it rests or sleeps. Dog houses that are elevated or situated on a platform protect the animal from cold and dampness that may seep through the ground. Of the breeds that are temperature hardy and will live outdoors, some are housed outside during the daytime only; others are permanent outdoor residents day and night, all year 'round.

If your intention is to have a companion that lives out-of-doors, it will be necessary to provide him with a more elaborate house, one that really protects him from the elements. Make sure the dog's house is constructed of waterproof materials. Furnish him with sufficient bedding to burrow into on a chilly night and provide extra insulation to keep out drafts and wet weather. Add a partition (a kind of room divider which separates the entry area from the main sleeping space) inside his house or attach a swinging door to the entrance to help keep him warm when he is inside his residence. The swinging door facilitates entry to and from the dog house, while at the same time it provides protection, particularly from wind and drafts.

Some fortunate owners whose yards are enclosed by high fencing allow their dogs complete freedom within the boundaries of their property. In these situations, a dog can leave his dog house and get all the exercise he wants. Of course such a large space requires more effort to keep it clean. An alternative to complete backyard freedom is a dog kennel or run which attaches to or surrounds the dog's house. This restricts some forms of movement, such as running, perhaps, but it does provide ample room for walking, climbing, jumping, and stretching. Another option is to fence off part of the yard and place the dog house in the enclosure. If you need to tether your dog to its house, make certain to use a fairly long lead so as not to hamper the animal's need to move and exercise his limbs.

A thick drape hung over the entrance to the dog's house will prevent drafts, thus keeping your dog warm and dry.

CLEANLINESS

No matter where your dog lives, either in or out of your home, be sure to keep him in surroundings that are as clean and sanitary as possible. His excrement should be removed and disposed of every day without fail. No dog should be forced to lie in his own feces. If your dog lives in his own house, the floor should be swept occasionally and the bedding should be changed regularly if it becomes soiled. Food and water dishes need to be scrubbed with hot water and detergent and rinsed well to remove all traces of soap. The water dish should be refilled with a supply of fresh water. The dog and his environment must be kept free of parasites (especially fleas and mosquitoes, which can carry disease) with products designed to keep these pests under control. Dog crates need frequent scrubbing, too, as do the floors of kennels and runs. Your pet must be kept clean and comfortable at all times; if you exercise strict sanitary control, you will keep disease and parasite infestation to a minimum.

Just as grooming and bathing keep your dog in a healthy condition, regular cleaning and disinfecting of his living area are important for his overall health. Many dogs that suffer from depression are subjected to

More and more cities and towns are requiring dog owners to clean up after their pets. Commercial pooper scoopers can make the clean-up easy and efficient. They are also helpful for backyard sanitation.

poorly maintained quarters. Your dog's physical and psychological well being are closely related. A clean dog is a healthy and happy dog.

Accommodations

EXERCISE

A well-balanced diet and regular medical attention from a qualified veterinarian are essential in promoting good health for your dog, but so is daily exercise to keep him fit and mentally alert. Dogs that have been confined all day while their owners are at work or school need special attention. There should be some time set aside make this daily ritual more pleasant both for themselves and their canine companions by combining the walk with a little "roughhousing," that is to say, a bit of fun and togetherness.

Whenever possible, take a stroll to an empty lot, a playground, or a nearby park. Attach a long lead to your dog's collar, and let him run and jump and tone his body through

Large outdoor pens are used by many breeding, boarding, and medical professionals. Always inspect the facility before leaving your dog in any professional's care.

each day for play—a romp with a family member, perhaps. Not everyone is lucky enough to let his dog run through an open meadow or along a sandy beach, but even a ten-minute walk in the fresh air will do. Dogs that are house-bound, particularly those that live in apartments, need to be walked out-of-doors after each meal so that they can relieve themselves. Owners can aerobic activity. This will help him burn calories and will keep him trim, and it will also help relieve tension and stress that may have had a chance to develop while you were away all day. For people who work Monday through Friday, weekend jaunts can be especially beneficial, since there will be more time to spend with your canine friend. You might

Responsible breeding practices, regular exercise, and proper nutrition all contribute to sound bone development.

want to engage him in a simple game of fetch with a stick or a rubber ball. Even such basic tricks as rolling over, standing on the hindlegs, or jumping up (all of which can be done inside the home as well) can provide additional exercise. But if you plan to challenge your dog with a real workout to raise his heart rate, remember not to push him too hard without first warming up with a brisk walk. Don't forget to "cool him down" afterwards with a rhythmic trot until his heart rate returns to normal. Some dog owners jog with their dogs or take them along on bicycle excursions.

At the very least, however, play with your dog every day to keep him in good shape physically and mentally. If you can walk him outdoors, or better yet run with him in a more vigorous activity, by all means do it. Don't neglect your pet and leave him confined

The knee joint is also known as the stifle joint. It is formed by the articulation of the upper and lower leg.

for long periods without attention from you or time for exercise.

EXERCISING FOR YOU AND YOUR DOG

Dogs are like people. They come in three weights: overweight, underweight, and the correct weight. It is fair to say that most dogs are in better shape than most humans who own them. The reason for this is that most dogs accept exercise without objection—people do not! Follow your dog's lead towards exercise and the complete enjoyment of the outdoors—your dog is the ideal work-out partner. There are toys at your local pet shop which are designed just for that purpose: to allow you to play and exercise with your dog. Here are a few recommended exercise toys for you and your dog.

Flying discs can make exercise exciting.

Frisbee® Flying Discs*

Who hasn't seen or heard of a Frisbee® flying disc? This flying-saucer–like toy is available in three or more sizes. The small size is 10 cm (4″); the medium size is about 15 cm (6″) and the larger size is 23 cm (9″). The size of the flying disc has little to do with the size of the dog—small puppies chase anything; some larger dogs chase nothing. The advantage of the larger disc is that it is the same size as the toy made for humans only! Start with the size that you think is best suited for your dog. What is much more important is the material from which the flying disc is made; *soft un-chew-worthy plastic flying discs are not good for dogs.*

Most people play with these polyethylene discs and use these same discs to play with their dogs. Polyethylene plastic discs usually last an hour or so. Every time the dog grabs it, his teeth dig into the cheap plastic, leaving an imprint. In a short while the disc is not useable— and even worse, it may be dangerous, since the dog can break off a chunk and swallow it, or the distorted disc can swerve out of control and hit someone.

*Frisbee® is a trademark of the Kransco Company, California, and is used for their brand of flying disc.

Be sure that you do not throw the flying disc where your dog can injure himself. Open spaces where cars are not permitted or a park are most ideal.

Nylon Discs

Your pet shop will have a nylon disc that has a dog bone molded into the top of it. While this may look silly at first, the advantage is simple. When a typical Frisbee® lands on a flat surface, the dog may be unable to grasp it with its mouth or turn it over with its paw. Thus frustrated, the dog loses interest in the game and you will have to fetch it yourself. The nylon disc with the bone molded into the top of it allows the dog the option of flipping it over with its paw or grasping it with its mouth. It also has more capacity; thus you can use it as a food or water dish on these outings. The nylon disc may also be flavored and scented, besides being annealed, so your dog can find it more easily if it gets lost in the woods or high grass.

Polyurethane Flexible Floppy Flying Discs

The greatest advance in flying discs came with the manufacture of these discs from polyurethane. The polyurethane is so soft that it doesn't hurt you, your dog, or the window it might strike accidentally. Only very, very rarely can it break a window—usually one that was already cracked. The polyurethane Gumadisc® is floppy and soft. It can be folded

Gumabone® flying discs are proven safe and durable for dogs. The soft, pliable texture and the scent impregnation make these discs loved by dogs.

and fits into your pocket. It is also much tougher than cheap plastics, and most pet shops guarantee that it will last ten times longer than cheap plastic discs.

With most flying discs made for dogs comes an instruction booklet on how to use the disc with your canine friend. Basically, you play with the dog and the disc so the dog knows the disc belongs to him. Then you throw it continuously, increasing the distance, so that the dog fetches it and brings it back to you.

The exercise for you comes in when your dog stops fetching it, or when you have a partner. The two of you play catch. You stand as far apart as available space allows—usually 30–35 m (100 feet) is more than enough room. You throw the disc to each other, arousing your dog's interest as he tries to catch it. When the disc is dropped or veers off, the dog grabs it and brings it back (hopefully). Obviously you will have to run to catch the disc before your dog does.

There are contests held all over the world where distance, height, and other characteristics are measured competitively. Ask your local pet shop to help you locate a Frisbee® Club near you.

*Frisbee® is a trademark of the Kransco Company, California, and is used for their brand of flying disc.

Many owners complain that plastic flying discs are destroyed quickly by their dogs, making an otherwise fun pastime an expensive outing. Flying discs made of annealed nylon are proven to last longer and thereby provide hours of enjoyable, affordable exercise for you and your dog.

Accommodations

Tug Toys

A tug toy is a hard rubber, cheap plastic, or polyurethane toy which allows a dog and his owner to have a game of tug-o-war. The owner grips one end while the dog grips the other—then they pull. The polyurethane flexible tug toy is the best on the market at the present time. Your pet shop will have one to show you. The polyurethane toys are clear in color and stay soft forever. Cheap plastic tug toys are indisputably dangerous, and the hard-rubber tug toys get brittle too fast and are too stiff for most dogs; however, there *is* a difference in price—just ask the advice of any shop operator.

Most every dog loves a challenging tug of war. Tug toys of sturdy polyurethane and strong cotton floss are favorites of many dogs.

Balls made of annealed nylon make fetching safe, pleasing and hygienic for your dog. Their virtually indestructible construction prevents the dog from tearing pieces of the ball and ingesting them, and the appealing scent inspires an enthusiastic retrieve. When worn, as shown here, nylon balls should be replaced with new ones.

Balls

Nobody has to tell you about playing ball with your dog. The reminder you may need is that you should not throw the ball where traffic might interfere with the dog's catching or fetching of it. The ball should not be cheap plastic (a dog's worst enemy as far as toys are concerned) but made of a substantial material. Balls made of nylon are practically indestructible, but they are very hard and must be rolled, never thrown. The same balls made of polyurethane are great—they bounce and are soft. The Nylabone® and Gumabone® balls are scented and flavored, and dogs can easily find them when lost.

Other manufacturers make balls of almost every substance, including plastic, cotton, and wood. Billiard balls, baseballs, tennis balls, and so on, have all been used by dog owners who want their dogs to play with them in a game of catch. A strong caveat is that you use only those balls made especially for dogs.

With the variety of safe, exercise-oriented chew products available, there is little excuse for a sedentary, plaque-infested existence to persist in an otherwise healthy dog.

Housebreaking and Training

Housebreaking can be the groundwork on which all future training is based. The two most commonly recommended methods involve paper training and crate training. When paper training is used, owners often employ litter boxes lined with paper to limit the area and make clean-up fast and easy.

HOUSEBREAKING

The new addition to your family may already have received some basic house training before his arrival in your home. If he has not, remember that a puppy will want to relieve himself about half a dozen times a day; it is up to you to specify where and when he should "do his business." Housebreaking is your first training concern and should begin the moment you bring the puppy home.

Ideally, puppies should be taken outdoors after meals, as a full stomach will exert pressure on the bladder and colon. What goes into the dog must eventually come out; the period after his meal is the most natural and appropriate time. When he eliminates, he should be praised, for this will increase the likelihood of the same thing happening after every meal. He should also be encouraged to use the same area and will probably be attracted to it after frequent use.

Some veterinarians maintain that a puppy can learn to urinate and defecate on command, if properly trained. The advantage of this conditioning technique is that your pet will associate the act of elimination with a particular word of your choice rather than with a particular time or place which might not always be convenient or available. So whether you are visiting an unfamiliar place or don't want to go outside with your dog in sub-zero temperatures, he will still be able to relieve himself when he hears the specific command word. Elimination will occur after this "trigger" phrase or word sets up a conditioned reflex in the dog, who will eliminate anything contained in his bladder or bowel upon hearing it. The shorter the word, the more you can repeat it and imprint it on your dog's memory.

Your chosen command word should be given simultaneously with the sphincter opening events in order to achieve perfect and rapid conditioning. This is why it is important to familiarize yourself with the tell-tale signs preceding your puppy's elimination process. Then you will be prepared to say the word at the crucial moment. There is usually a sense of urgency on the dog's part; he may follow a sniffing and circling pattern which you will soon recognize. It is important to use the command in his usual area only when you know the puppy

can eliminate, i.e., when his stomach or bladder is full. He will soon learn to associate the act with the word. One word of advice, however, if you plan to try out this method: never use the puppy's name or any other word which he might frequently hear about the house—you can imagine the result!

Finally, remember that any training takes time. Such a conditioned response can be obtained with intensive practice with any normal, healthy dog over six weeks of age. Even Pavlov's salivating dogs required fifty repetitions before the desired response was achieved. Patience and persistence will eventually produce results—do not lose heart!

Indoors, sheets of newspapers can be used to cover the specific area where your dog should relieve himself. These should be placed some distance away from his sleeping and feeding area, as a puppy will not urinate or defecate where he eats. When the newspapers are changed, the bottom papers should be placed on top of the new ones in order to reinforce the purpose of the papers by scent as well as by sight. The puppy should be praised during or immediately after he has made use of this particular part of the room. Each positive reinforcement increases the possibility of his using that area again.

When he arrives, it is advisable to limit the puppy to one room, usually the kitchen, as it most likely has a linoleum or easily washable floor surface. Given the run of the house, the sheer size of the place will seem overwhelming and confusing and he might leave his "signature"

PATIENCE, PERSISTENCE, AND PRAISE

As with a human baby, you must be patient, tolerant, and understanding of your pet's mistakes, making him feel loved and wanted, not rejected and isolated. You wouldn't hit a baby for soiling his diapers, as you

An anchored lead can be the solution to a yard without a fence.

on your furniture or clothes! There will be time later to familiarize him gradually with his new surroundings.

would realize that he was not yet able to control his bowel movements; be as compassionate with your canine infant. Never rub his nose in his excreta. Never indulge in the common practice of punishing him with a rolled-up newspaper. Never hit a puppy with your hand. He will only become "hand-shy" and learn to fear you. Usually the punishment is meted out sometime after the offense and loses its efficacy, as the bewildered dog cannot connect the two events. Moreover, by association, he will soon learn to be afraid of you and anything to do with newspapers—including, perhaps, that area where he is *supposed* to relieve himself!

Most puppies are eager to please. Praise, encouragement, and reward (particularly the food

From the moment you bring your dog home, the rules of the house must be enforced to ensure a consistently obedient home companion.

variety) will produce far better results than any scolding or physical punishment. Moreover, it is far better to dissuade your puppy from doing certain things, such as chewing on chair legs or other furniture, by making those objects particularly distasteful to him. Some pet shops stock bitter apple sprays or citronella compounds for application to furniture legs. If these are ineffective, you could smear them with a generous amount of hot chili sauce or cayenne pepper mixed with petroleum jelly, for example. This would make it seem as if the object itself was administering the

Professionals cite that housebreaking on newspapers can cause some dogs to believe that it is always okay to excrete on papers, regardless of location. Housebreaking pads are used by many cautious owners.

punishment whenever he attempted to chew it. He probably wouldn't need a second reminder!

Remember that the reason a dog has housebreaking or behavior problems is because his owner has allowed them to develop. This is why you must begin as you intend to continue, letting your dog know what is acceptable and unacceptable behavior. It is also important that you be consistent in your demands; you cannot feed him from the dining room table one day and then punish him when he begs for food from your dinner guests.

TRAINING

You will want the newest member of your family to be welcomed by everyone; this will not happen if he urinates in every room of the house or barks all night! He needs training in the correct forms of behavior in this new human world. You cannot expect your puppy to become the perfect pet overnight. He needs your help in his socialization process. Training greatly facilitates and enhances the relationship of the dog to his owner and to the rest of society. A successfully trained dog can

Housebreaking and Training

be taken anywhere and behave well with anyone. Indeed, it is that one crucial word—*training*—which can transform an aggressive animal into a peaceful, well-behaved pet. Now, how does this "transformation" take place?

Some owners of small dogs use a figure-eight-style harness as a means of restraint.

Collars should always be worn, with identification tag and license attached.

WHEN AND HOW TO TRAIN

Like housebreaking, training should begin as soon as the puppy enters the house. The formal training sessions should be short but frequent, for example, ten to fifteen minute periods three times a day. These are much more effective than long, tiring sessions of half an hour which might soon become boring. You are building your relationship with your puppy during these times, so make them as enjoyable as possible. It is a good idea to have these sessions *before* the puppy's meal, not after it when he wouldn't feel like exerting himself; the dog will then associate something pleasurable with his training sessions and look forward to them.

THE COLLAR AND LEASH

Your puppy should become used to a collar and leash as soon as possible. If he is very

The variety of canine collars and leashes available surely allows for the personal touch.

young, a thin, choke-chain collar can be used, but you will need a larger and heavier one for training when he is a little older. Remember to have his name and address on an identification tag attached to his collar, as you don't want to lose your pet if he

A choke collar can be an effective training tool when used properly.

should happen to leave your premises and explore the neighborhood!

Let the puppy wear his collar until he is used to how it feels. After a short time he will soon become accustomed to it and you can attach the leash. He might resist your attempts to lead him or simply sit down and refuse to budge. Fight him for a few minutes, tugging on the leash if necessary, then let him relax for the day. He won't be trained until he learns that he must obey the pull under any circumstance, but this will take a few sessions. Remember that a dog's period of concentration is short, so LITTLE and OFTEN is the wisest course of action—and

patience is the password to success.

GIVING COMMANDS

When you begin giving your puppy simple commands, make them as short as possible and use the same word with the same meaning at all times, for example, "Heel," "Sit," and "Stay." You must be consistent; otherwise your puppy will become confused. The dog's name should prefix all commands to attract his attention. Do not become impatient with him however many times you have to repeat your command.

A good way to introduce the "Come" command is by calling the puppy when his meal is ready. Once this is learned, you can call your pet to you at will, always remembering to praise him for his prompt obedience. This "reward," or positive reinforcement, is such a crucial part of training that a Director of the New York Academy of Dog Training constructed his whole teaching program upon the methods of "Love, Praise, and Reward." Incidentally, if you use the command "Come," use it every time. Don't switch to "Come here" or "Come boy," as this will only confuse your dog.

It is worth underlining the fact that punishment is an ineffective teaching technique. We have already seen this in housebreaking. For example, if your pup should run away, it

A puppy's collar should be light and comfortable, yet still effectively secure the dog.

would be senseless to beat him when he eventually returns; he would only connect the punishment with his return, not with running away! In addition, it is unwise to call him to you to punish him, as he will soon learn not to respond when you call his name.

A lead that allows for a sure, comfortable grip is a training necessity. Introduce your new dog to the lead slowly. When he becomes comfortable with it, training can begin.

SOME SPECIFIC COMMANDS

"Sit" This is one of the easiest and most useful commands for your dog to learn, so it is a good idea to begin with it. The only equipment required is a leash, a collar, and a few tasty tidbits. Take your dog out for some exercise before his meal. After about five minutes, call him to you, praise him when he arrives,

A popular item with owners who love to walk their dogs is the harness. The harness fits comfortably around the dog's forequarters and displaces the pressure of the owner's tug on the lead.

and slip his collar on him. Hold the leash tightly in your right hand; this should force the dog's head up and focus his attention on you. As you say "Sit" in a loud, clear voice, with your left hand press steadily on his rump until he is in a sitting position. As soon as he is in the correct position, praise him and give him the tidbit you have in your hand. Now wait a few minutes to let him rest and repeat the routine. Through repetition, the dog soon associates the word with the act. Never make the lesson too long. Eventually your praise will be reward enough for your puppy. Other methods to teach this command exist, but this one, executed with care and moderation, has proven the most effective.

"Sit-Stay/Stay" To teach your pet to remain in one place or "stay" on your command, first of all order him to the sitting position at your side. Lower your left hand with the flat of your palm in front of his nose and your fingers pointing downwards. Hold the leash high and taut behind his head so that he cannot move. Speak the command "Sit-stay" and, as you are giving it, step in front of him. Repeat the command and tighten the leash so the animal cannot follow you. Walk completely around him, repeating the command and keeping him motionless by holding the leash at arm's length above him to check his movement. When he remains in this position for about fifteen seconds, you can begin the second part of the training. You will have to exchange the leash for a nylon cord or rope about twenty to thirty feet long. Repeat the whole routine from the beginning and be ready to prevent any movement towards you with a sharp "Sit-stay." Move around him in ever-widening circles until you are about fifteen feet away from him. If he still remains seated, you can pat yourself on the back! One useful thing to remember is that the dog makes associations with what you say, how you say it, and what you do while you are saying it. Give this command in a firm, clear tone of voice, perhaps using an admonishing forefinger raised, warning the dog to "stay."

Two training accessories especially common with obedience trial enthusiasts are the hurdle (above) and the dumbbell (below). To see dogs performing with these and other field accessories, attend an obedience competition. Remember that training requires consistency and commitment, but the rewards are well worth the effort.

"Heel" When you walk your dog, you should hold the leash firmly in your right hand. The dog should walk on your left so you have the leash crossing your body. This enables you to have greater control over the dog.

Let your dog lead you for the first few moments so that he fully understands that freedom can be his if he goes about it properly. He already knows that when he wants to go outdoors the leash and collar are necessary, so he has respect for the leash. Now, if he starts to pull in one direction while walking, all you do is *stop walking.* He will walk a few steps and then find that he can't walk any further. He will then turn and look into your face. *This is the crucial point!* Just stand there for a moment and stare right back at him . . . now walk another ten feet and stop again. Again your dog will probably walk to the end of the leash, find he can't go any further, and turn around and look again. If he starts to pull and jerk, just stand there. After he quiets down, bend down and comfort him, as he may be frightened. Keep up this training until he learns not to outwalk you.

Once the puppy obeys the pull of the leash, half of your training is accomplished. "Heeling" is a necessity for a well-behaved dog, so teach him to walk beside you, head even with your knee.

Nothing looks sadder than a big dog taking his helpless owner for a walk. It is annoying to passers-by and other dog owners to have a large dog, however friendly, bear down on them and entangle dogs, people, and packages.

To teach your dog, start off walking briskly, saying "Heel" in a firm voice. Pull back with a sharp jerk if he lunges ahead, and if he lags repeat the command and tug on the leash, not allowing him to drag behind. After the dog has learned to heel at various speeds on leash, you

The lead is an essential tool for teaching such commands as "heel," "come," and "down."

can remove it and practice heeling free, but have it ready to snap on again as soon as he wanders.

"Come" Your dog has already learned to come to you when you call his name. Why? Because you only call him when his food is ready or when you wish to play with him or praise him. Outdoors such a response is more difficult to achieve, if he is happily playing by himself or with other dogs, so he must be trained to come to you when he is called. To teach him to come, let him reach the end of a long lead, then give the command, gently pulling him towards you at the same time. As soon as he associates the word *come* with the action of moving towards you, pull only when he does not respond immediately. As he starts to come, move back to make him learn that he must come from a distance as well as when he is close to you. Soon you may be able to practice without a leash, but if he is slow to come or actively disobedient, go to him and pull him toward you, repeating the command. Always remember to reward his successful completion of a task.

"Down" Teaching the "down" command ideally begins while your dog is still a pup. During puppyhood your dog frequently will lie down, as this position is one of the dog's most natural positions. Invest some time, and keep close watch over your pup. Each time he begins to lie, repeat in a low convincing tone the word "down." If for the first day of training, you concur a majority of the dog's sitting with your commands and continue with reinforcement and moderate praise your pup should conquer the "down" command in no time.

Teaching the "down" command to a mature dog likely will require more effort. Although the lying position is still natural to a dog, his being forced into it is not. Some dogs may react with fear, anger, or confusion. Others may accept the process and prove quick learners. Have your

For the dog that responds with anger or aggression, attach a lead (and a muzzle) and have the dog sit facing you at a close distance. There should be a J-loop formed by the lead. With moderate force, relative to the size and strength of your dog, step on the J-loop, forcing the dog down, while repeating the command "down" in a low forceful tone. When the dog is down, moderate praise should

Threats and physical punishment have no place in the canine training process. The keys to effective training are patience, persistence, and praise.

dog sit and face you. If he is responsive and congenial, gently take his paws, and slowly pull them towards you; give the "down" command as he approaches the proper position. Repeat several times: moderate reinforcement of this procedure should prove rewardingly successful.

be given. If the dog proves responsive, you may attempt extending his legs to the "down" position—leaving the muzzle on, of course. Daily reinforcement of the training method will soon yield the desired results. The keys to remember are: patience, persistence, and praise.

Behavior Modification

"Problems with the Barking Dog" and "Aggressive Behavior and Dominance" reprinted with permission from *Canine Practice*, April 1977 (Volume 4, Number 2), pages 8–15. Published by Veterinary Practice Publishing Company, Santa Barbara, California.

PROBLEMS WITH THE BARKING DOG

One of the most frequent complaints about canine behavior is barking. Aside from the biting dog, the barking dog is probably the pet peeve of many non-dog owners. I know of at least one city in which owners of dogs that bark excessively, and for which there are complaints on file, are required to take steps to eliminate the barking.

Canine practitioners are drawn into problems with barking when they are asked for their advice in helping an owner come up with a solution or, as a last resort, when they are requested to perform a debarking operation or even euthanasia. In this column I will deal with some of the factors that apparently cause dogs to bark and suggest some corrective approaches.

Barking is, of course, a natural response for many dogs. They have an inherited predisposition to bark as an alarm when other dogs or people approach their territory. Alarm barking makes

A problem facing many dog owners is excessive vocalization. Fortunately, a number of correctives have proven successful.

many dogs valuable as household watchdogs and is not necessarily undesirable behavior. With a different vocal tone and pattern, dogs bark when they are playing with each other. On occasion dogs have a tendency to bark back at other dogs or join in with other barking dogs.

In addition to inherited barking tendencies, dogs can also learn to bark if the barking is followed, at least sometimes, by a reward. Thus dogs may bark when they wish to come in the house or to get out of a kennel. Some dogs are trained to bark upon hearing the command "speak" for a food reward.

One of the first approaches to

take when discussing a barking problem is to determine if the behavior is a manifestation of a natural (inherited) tendency or is learned behavior which has been rewarded in the past.

Can Barking Be Extinguished? Extinction, as a way of eliminating a behavioral problem, may be considered when it is clear that the behavior has been learned and when one can identify the specific rewarding or reinforcing factors that maintain the behavior.

For example, the dog that barks upon hearing the command "speak" is periodically rewarded with food and praise. If a dog is never, ever given food or praise again when it barks after being told to "speak," it will eventually stop this type of barking. This is the process of extinction and it implies that the

Reward in the form of treats is often effective.

behavior must be repeated but never again rewarded.

A more practical example of the possible use of extinction would be in dealing with the dog that apparently barks because, at least occasionally, it is allowed in the house. By not allowing the dog in the house until the barking has become very frequent and loud, the owners may have shaped the barking behavior to that which is the most objectionable. If the dog is never allowed in the house again when barking, the barking should eventually be extinguished—at least theoretically.

How Should Punishment Be Used? Sometimes it is not feasible to attempt to extinguish barking even if it seems to be the case that the behavior was learned. This brings up the advisability of punishment. Clients who seek advice in dealing with a barking problem may already have employed some type of punishment such as shouting at the dog or throwing something at it. That this type of punishment is ineffective is attested to by the fact that the client is seeking advice. By shouting at a dog or hitting, a person interferes with what effect the punishment may have on the behavior itself through the arousal of autonomic reactions and escape attempts or submissive responses by the dog.

The Water Bucket Approach

I am rather impressed by the ingenuity of some dog owners in coming up with ways to punish a dog for barking without being directly involved in administering the punishment. One such harried dog owner I talked to, who was also a veterinarian, was plagued by his dog's barking in the kennel commencing at about 1:30 a.m. every night. A platform to hold a bucket of water was constructed over the area of the kennel in which the dog usually chose to bark. Through a system of hinges, ropes, and pulleys, a mechanism was devised so that the dog owner could pull a rope from his bedroom window, dumping a bucket of water on the dog when he started to bark. The bucket was suspended such that once it was dumped, it uprighted itself and the owner could fill it again remotely by turning on a garden hose. After two appropriate dunkings, the dog's barking behavior was apparently eliminated.

With a little ingenuity, a bucket attached to a trap door can be constructed. Soaking the dog in this surprising manner can possibly extinguish a bad barking habit. Always take into consideration the weather conditions, the health and age of your dog, and the cause of the barking problem before embarking on the water-bucket cure.

In advising a client on the type of punishment discussed above, keep in mind one important consideration. From the time the owner is ready to administer punishment for barking, every attempt should be made to punish all undesirable barking from that point on and not to allow excessively long periods of barking to go unpunished. Thus it may be necessary to keep a dog indoors when away unless the dog will be punished for barking when the owner is gone.

Behavior Modification

Alternative Responses Barking dogs are, and probably always will be, one of the enduring problems of dog owners. Barking is relatively effortless, and it is such a natural response for many dogs that it is admittedly hard to eliminate with either punishment or a program of conditioning non-barking. In some instances it may be advisable to forget about eliminating barking and to suggest that the problem be dealt with by changing the circumstances which lead to barking. For example, a dog that barks continuously in the backyard while the owners are away may not bark if left in the house while they are gone. But the problem of keeping the dog in the house may be related to inadequate house training or the dog's shedding hair or climbing onto the furniture. It may be easier to correct these latter behavioral problems than it is to change the barking behavior.

Especially for aggressive dogs, muzzles can prevent both injuries and lawsuits.

AGGRESSIVE BEHAVIOR AND DOMINANCE

Aggressiveness can have many causes. Determining what kind of aggression an animal is manifesting is a prerequisite to successful treatment of the behavior. A frequent problem that is presented to the practitioner is one of aggression related to dominance.

Dogs, which are social animals, have a hierarchal system of dominance within their pack. This predisposition to take a dominant or submissive position relative to fellow canines also occurs in relationship to people. Only in unusual situations would a submissive dog threaten a dominant animal, and almost never would it physically assault its superior. The dominant dog, however, frequently threatens submissive individuals to maintain its position. In a household setting, a person may be the object of threats, and when the person backs off, the dog's position is reassured. The aggressive behavior is also reinforced, and when behavior is reinforced it is likely to recur.

Case History The following is a typical case history of a dog presented for aggression stemming from dominance.

Max was a two-year-old intact male Cocker Spaniel. He had been acquired by Mr. Smith, one year prior to his owner's marriage, as a puppy. He liked and was well liked by both Mr. and Mrs. Smith. He frequently solicited and received attention from both people. However, several times over the last few months, Max had snapped at Mrs. Smith and repeatedly growled at her. A detailed anamnesis revealed that such incidents usually occurred in situations where the dog wanted his own way or did not want to be bothered. He would growl if asked to move off a chair or if persistently commanded to do a specific task. He growled if Mrs. Smith came between him and a young female Cocker Spaniel acquired a year ago. He also refused to let Mrs. Smith take anything from his possession.

Behavior Modification

Max never showed any of these aggressive behaviors toward Mr. Smith or strangers. Admittedly he did not have much opportunity to demonstrate such behaviors toward strangers. A description of the dog's body and facial postures and circumstances under which the

Dogs can become possessive of their playthings or aggressive in defense of their territory.

aggression occurred did not indicate that this was a case of fear-induced aggression, but rather one of assertion of dominance.

Mrs. Smith's reaction to the aggression was always to retreat, and, hence, the dog was rewarded for his assertiveness. She had never physically disciplined the dog and was afraid to do so. To encourage her to physically take control of the dog would likely have resulted in her being bitten. The dominance-submissive relationship had to be reversed in a more subtle manner.

Instructions to Client Mrs. Smith was instructed to avoid all situations which might evoke any aggressive signs from Max. This was to prevent any further reinforcement of his growling and threats.

Both she and her husband were not to indiscriminately pet or show affection towards the dog. For the time being, if Max solicited attention from Mr. Smith, he was to ignore the dog. Mrs. Smith was to take advantage of Max's desire for attention by giving him a command which he had to obey before she praised and petted him. She was also to take advantage of high motivation levels for other activities whenever such situations arose. Max had to obey a command before she gave him anything—

before she petted him, before she let him out or in, etc.

Mrs. Smith also was to assume total care of the dog and become "the source of all good things in life" for Max. She was to feed him, take him on walks, play with him, etc.

Mrs. Smith also spent 5–10 minutes a day teaching Max simple parlor tricks and obedience responses for coveted food rewards as well as praise. These were entirely fun and play sessions—but within a few days the dog had acquired the habit of quickly responding to commands. And this habit transferred over to the non-game situations.

Results Within a few weeks,

The dog's bed can become an object of possession. The dog can come to perceive it as his territory, not allowing others to come near. In such instances behavior modification may be necessary.

Max had ceased to growl and threaten Mrs. Smith in situations that he previously had. He would move out of her way or lie quietly when she would pass by him. She could order him off the furniture and handle the female Cocker Spaniel without eliciting threats from Max.

Mrs. Smith still felt that she would not be able to take the objects from Max's possession. Additional instructions were

A dog comes to associate the pleasure of receiving a treat with the action immediately preceding it. Treats are effective in shaping behavior and building a relationship with your pet when they are used judiciously and in moderation.

given to her. She then began placing a series of objects at progressively closer distances to the dog while the dog was in a sit-stay position. After she placed the object on the floor for a short time, she would pick it up. If the dog was still in a sit-stay (which it always was), he received a reward of cheese and verbal praise. Eventually the objects were to be placed and

removed from directly in front of the dog. At first she was to use objects that the dog did not care much about and then progressively use more coveted items. This was what she was supposed to do, but before she actually had completed the program she called in excitedly to report that she had taken a piece of stolen food and a household ornament from Max's mouth. And he didn't even object! She said she had calmly told Max to sit. He did. He was so used to doing so, in the game and other situations, that the response was now automatic. She walked over, removed the item from his mouth, and praised him.

Mrs. Smith did resume the systematic presentation of objects and put the dog on an intermittent schedule of food and praise reinforcement during the practice sessions. Mr. Smith again began interacting with Max.

A progress check six months later indicated Max was still an obedient dog and had definitely assumed a submissive position relative to both of his owners. The dominance hierarchy between Max and Mrs. Smith had been reversed *without resorting to any physical punishment.* Mrs. Smith was instructed to reinforce her dominance position by frequently giving Max a command and reinforcing him for the appropriate response.

Summary The essential elements in treatment of such cases are as follows. First, of course, there must be a correct diagnosis of what kind of aggressive behavior is occurring. During the course of treatment, the submissive person(s) should avoid all situations that might evoke an aggressive attitude by the dog. All other family members should totally ignore the dog during the treatment interim. The person most dominated by the dog should take over complete care of the dog in addition to spending 5–10 minutes a day teaching the dog tricks or simple obedience commands (sit-stay is a useful one to gain control of the dog in subsequent circumstances). These should be fun-and-games situations. Food rewards are highly recommended in addition to simple praise.

The person submissive to the dog should take the opportunity to give the dog a command, which must be obeyed, before doing anything pleasant for the dog.

It must be emphasized to the owner that no guarantee can be made that the dog will never threaten or be aggressive again. What is being done, as with all other aggression cases, is an attempt to reduce the likelihood, incidence, and intensity of occurrence of the aggressive behavior.

DESTRUCTIVE TENDENCIES

It is ironical but true that a dog's destructive behavior in the home may be proof of his love for his owner. He may be trying to get more attention from his owner or, in other cases, may be expressing his frustration at his owner's absence. An abundance

Some crates have wire-mesh fronts while others do not. The primary consideration in choosing a crate is its ventilation.

of unused energy may also contribute to a dog's destructive behavior, and therefore the owner should ensure that his dog has, at least, twenty minutes of vigorous exercise a day.

As a dog's destructive tendencies may stem from his desire to get more attention from his owner, the latter should devote specific periods each day to his dog when he is actively interacting with him. Such a period should contain practice obedience techniques during which the owner can reward the dog with his favorite food as well as praise and affection.

Planned departure conditioning is one specific technique which has been used to solve the problem of destructive tendencies in a puppy. It eventually ensures the dog's good behavior during the owner's absence. A series of

Not just great recreational devices to channel doggie tensions, the Gumabone® products have been scientifically proven to reduce tartar and plaque build-up. These products are available in many shapes and sizes. Gumabone® products should be replaced regularly when they become excessively worn.

short departures, which are identical to real departures, should condition the dog to behave well in the owner's absence. How is this to be achieved? Initially, the departures are so short (2–5 minutes) that the dog has no opportunity to be destructive. The dog is always rewarded for having been good when the owner returns. Gradually the duration of the departures is increased. The departure time is also varied so that the dog does not know when the owner is going to return. Since a different kind of behavior is now expected, it is best if a new stimulus or "atmosphere" is introduced into the training sessions to permit the dog to distinguish these departures as different from previous departures when he was destructive.

This new stimulus could be the sound of the radio or television. The association which the dog will develop is that whenever the "signal" or "stimulus" is on, the owner will return in an unknown

A proven safe chew product.

A safe tug toy.

period of time and, if the dog has not been destructive, he will be rewarded. As with the daily owner-dog interaction, the food reward is especially useful.

If the dog misbehaves during his owner's absence, the owner should speak sternly to him and isolate him from social contact for at least thirty minutes. (Puppies hate to be ignored.) Then the owner should conduct another departure of a shorter time and generously reward good behavior when he returns. The owner should progress slowly enough in the program so that once the departure has been initiated, the dog is never given an opportunity to make a mistake.

If planned departures are working satisfactorily, the departure time may gradually be extended to several hours. To reduce the dog's anxiety when left alone, he should be given a "safety valve" such as the indestructible Nylabone® to play with and chew on.

Health Care

From the moment you purchase your puppy, the most important person in both your lives becomes your veterinarian. His professional advice and treatment will ensure the good health of your pet. The vet is the first person to call when illness or accidents occur. Do *not* try to be your own veterinarian or apply human remedies to canine diseases. However, just as you would keep a first aid kit handy for minor injuries sustained by members of your family at home, so you should keep a similar kit prepared for your pet.

First aid for your dog would consist of stopping any bleeding, cleaning the wound, and

Even in your own back yard, injuries can occur.

preventing infection. Thus your kit might contain medicated powder, gauze bandages, and adhesive tape to be used in case of cuts. If the cut is deep and bleeding profusely, the bandage should be applied very tightly to help in the formation of a clot. A tight bandage should not be kept in place longer than necessary, so take your pet to the veterinarian immediately.

Walking or running on a cut pad prevents the cut from healing. Proper suturing of the cut and regular changing of the bandages should have your pet's wound healed in a week to ten days. A minor cut should be covered with a light bandage, for you want as much air as possible to reach the wound. Do not apply wads of cotton to a wound; they will stick to the area and may cause contamination.

You should also keep some hydrogen peroxide available, as it is useful in cleaning wounds and is also one of the best and simplest emetics known. Cotton applicator swabs are useful for applying ointment or removing debris from the eyes. A pair of tweezers should also be kept handy for removing foreign bodies from the dog's neck, head or body.

Nearly everything a dog might contract in the way of sickness has basically the same set of symptoms: loss of appetite, diarrhea, dull eyes, dull coat,

When emergencies occur, it pays to be prepared. A first-aid kit, well stocked with common sense medical accessories and tools, is helpful to have available at all times.

warm and/or runny nose, and a high temperature. Therefore, it is most important to take his temperature at the first sign of illness. To do this, you will need a rectal thermometer which should be lubricated with petroleum jelly. Carefully insert it into the rectum, holding it in place for at least two minutes. It must be held firmly; otherwise there is the danger of its being sucked up into the rectum or slipping out, thus giving an inaccurate reading. The normal temperature for a dog is between 101° and 102.5°F. If your pet is seriously ill or injured in an accident, your veterinarian will advise you what to do before he arrives.

Health Care

SWALLOWING FOREIGN OBJECTS

Most of us have had experience with a child swallowing a foreign object. Usually it is a small coin; occasionally it may be a fruit pit or something more dangerous. Dogs, *as a general rule,* will not swallow anything which isn't edible. There are, however, many dogs that swallow pebbles or small shiny objects such as pins, coins, and bits of cloth and plastic. This is especially true of dogs that are offered so-called "chew toys."

Chew toys are available in many sizes, shapes, colors and materials. Some even have whistles which sound when the dog's owner plays with it or when the dog chomps on it quickly. Most dogs attack the whistle first, doing everything possible to make it stop squeaking. Obviously, if the whistle is made of metal, a dog can injure its mouth, teeth, or tongue. Therefore, *never* buy a "squeak toy" made with a metal whistle.

Other chew toys are made of vinyl, a cheap plastic which is soft to the touch and pliable. Most of the cute little toys that are figures of animals or people are made of this cheap plastic. They are sometimes hand-painted in countries where the cost of such labor is low. Not only is the paint used dangerous to dogs, because of the lead content, but the vinyl tears easily and is usually destroyed by the dog during the first hour. Small bits of vinyl may be ingested and cause blockage of the intestines. You are, therefore, reminded of these things before you buy anything vinyl for your dog!

Very inexpensive dog toys, usually found in supermarkets and other low-price venues, may be made of polyethylene. These are to be avoided completely, as this cheap plastic is, for some odd reason, attractive to dogs. Dogs destroy the toy in minutes and sometimes swallow the indigestible bits and pieces that come off. Most pet shops carry only safe toys.

WHAT TOYS ARE SAFE FOR DOGS?

Hard Rubber Toys made of hard rubber are usually safe for dogs, providing the toy is made of 100% hard rubber and not a compound of rubber and other materials. The rubber must be "virgin" and not re-ground from old tires, tubes, and other scrap rubber products. The main problem with rubber, even 100% virgin rubber, is that it oxidizes quickly, especially when subjected to the ultraviolet rays of the sun and a dog's saliva. The rubber then tends to be brittle, to crack, to dust off, and to be extremely dangerous to dogs that like swallowing things.

From top to bottom, *the four common bite types are: (a) level, (b) scissors, (c) undershot, and (d) overshot. Different breeds have different bite types and one bite type may be desirable in your breed and most undesirable in another.*

Nylon Toys Toys made of nylon could well be the safest of all toys, *providing the nylon is annealed.* Nylon that is not annealed is very fragile ,and if you smash it against a hard surface, it might shatter like glass. The same is true when the weather is cold and the nylon drops below freezing. Thus far there is only one line of dog toys that is made of annealed virgin nylon—Nylabone®. These toys are not only annealed but they are flavored and scented. The flavors and scents, such as hambone, are undetectable by humans, but dogs seem to find them attractive.

Some nylon bones have the flavor sprayed on them or molded into them. These cheaper bones are easy to detect—just smell them. If you discern an odor, you know they are poorly made. The main

The inherent need to chew is strong in dogs of all ages. The canine's constant chewing of his favorite chew products will necessitate their regular replacement. When a bone becomes frayed, it's time to replace it.

problem with the nylon toys that have an odor is that they are not annealed and they "smell up" the house or car. The dog's saliva dilutes the odor of the bone, and when he drops it on your rug, this odor attaches itself to the rug and is quite difficult to remove.

Annealed nylon may be the best there is ,but it is not 100% safe. The Nylabone® dog chews are really meant to be Pooch Pacifiers®. This trade name indicates the effect intended for the dog, which is to relieve the tension in your excited puppy or adult dog who is left alone or wants to "spite" you. Instead of chewing up the furniture or some other object, he chews up his Nylabone® instead. Many dogs ignore the Nylabone® for weeks, suddenly attacking it when they have to relieve their doggie tensions.

Some dogs may have jaws strong enough to chomp off a piece of Nylabone®, but this is extremely rare. *One word of caution:* the Nylabone® should be replaced when the dog has chewed down the knuckle. Most dogs slowly scrape off small slivers of nylon which pass harmlessly through their digestive tract. The resultant frizzled bone actually becomes a toothbrush.

One of the great characteristics of nylon bones is that they can be boiled and

The Gumaknot® is the favorite chew item of many dogs.

Above: *The Nylabone® is an effective, proven-safe therapeutic device.* **Below**: *The Gumaball® is useful for outside recreation, exercise, and tooth care.*

Doggie treats come in a wide variety of sizes, shapes, and flavors. While they can be useful as rewards and occasional tidbits, they do not satisfy the dog's need to chew. Treats are best used for what they are intended—as treats.

sterilized. If a dog loses interest in his Nylabone®, or it is too hard for him to chew due to his age and the condition of his teeth, you can cook it in some chicken or beef broth, allowing it to boil for 30 minutes. Let it cool down normally. It will then be perfectly sterile and re-flavored for the next dog. *Don't try this with plastic bones, as they will melt and ruin your pot.*

Polyurethane Toys Toys made of polyurethane are almost as good as nylon bones—but not quite. There are several brands on the market: ignore the ones which have scents that you can discern. Some of the scented polyurethane bones have an unbearable odor after the scent has rubbed off the bone and onto your rug or car seat. Again, look for the better-quality polyurethane toy. Gumabone® is

a flexible material, the same as used for making artificial hearts and the bumpers on automobiles, thus it is strong and stable. It is not as strong as Nylabone®, but many dogs like it because it is soft.

The most popular of the Gumabone® products made in polyurethane are the tug toys, balls, and Frisbee® flying discs. These items are almost clear in color, have the decided advantage of lasting a long time, and are useful in providing exercise for both a dog and his master or mistress.

Whatever dog toy you buy, be sure it is high quality. Pet shops, as a rule, carry the better-quality toys, while supermarkets seem to be concerned only with price. Of course there may be exceptions, but you are best advised to ask your local pet shop operator—or even your veterinarian—what toys are suitable for *your* dog.

In conclusion, if your dog is a swallower of foreign objects, don't give him anything cheap to chew on. If he swallows a coin, you can hardly blame the Treasury! Unless your dog is carefully supervised, use only the largest size Nylabone®, and replace it as soon as the dog chews down the knuckles. *Do not let the dog take the Nylabone® outdoors.* First of all he can hide and bury it, digging it up when his tensions rise. Then, too, all nylon becomes more brittle when it freezes, even Nylabone®.

IF YOUR PET SWALLOWS POISON

A poisoned dog must be treated instantly; any delay could cause his death. Different poisons act in different ways and require different treatments. If you know the dog has swallowed an acid, alkali, gasoline, or kerosene, do not induce vomiting. Give milk to dilute the poison and rush him to the vet. If you can find the bottle or container of poison, check the label to see if there is a recommended antidote. If not, try to induce vomiting by giving him a mixture of hydrogen peroxide and water. Mix the regular drugstore strength of hydrogen peroxide (3%) with an equal part of water, but do not attempt to pour it down your dog's throat, as that could cause inhalation pneumonia. Instead, simply pull the dog's lips away from the side of his mouth, making a pocket for depositing the liquid. Use at least a tablespoonful of the mixture for every ten pounds of your dog's

Handling a dog who is sick or injured requires skill. To protect yourself from being bitten, you should first secure the dog's muzzle with a slow, cautious motion, if no safety muzzle is available. Then the animal can be treated or transported as required.

weight. He will vomit in about two minutes. When his stomach has settled, give him a teaspoonful of Epsom salts in a little water to empty the intestine quickly. The hydrogen peroxide, on ingestion, becomes oxygen and water and is harmless to your dog; it is the best antidote for phosphorus, which is often used in rat poisons. After you have administered this emergency treatment to your pet and his stomach and bowels have been emptied, rush him to your veterinarian for further care.

DANGER IN THE HOME

There are numerous household products that can prove fatal if ingested by your pet. These include rat poison, antifreeze, boric acid, hand soap, detergents, insecticides, mothballs, household cleansers,

Water hemlock is one of the many poisonous plants that can cause serious complications if ingested by a canine.

bleaches, de-icers, polishes and disinfectants, paint and varnish removers, acetone, turpentine, and even health and beauty aids if ingested in large enough quantities. A word to the wise should be sufficient: what you would keep locked away from your two-year-old child should also be kept hidden from your pet.

There is another danger lurking within the home among the household plants, which are almost all poisonous, even if swallowed in small quantities. There are hundreds of poisonous plants around us, among which are: ivy leaves, cyclamen, lily of the valley, rhododendrons, tulip bulbs, azalea, wisteria, poinsettia

Suburban backyards are often fertile grounds for a variety of flowering plant types. Many of these pretty-to-the-eye plants can be harmful to a canine. Lily-of-the-valley is attractive and popular in some climates; it is, however, poisonous if ingested and should not be cultivated near the dog's living area.

Lactrodectus mactans, better known as the black widow spider, is said to possess venom over 15 times as toxic as many rattlesnakes'. This spider most commonly occurs in warm climates. Owners are encouraged to inspect the dog's living area periodically for such lethal inhabitants.

leaves, mistletoe, daffodils, delphiniums, foxglove leaves, the jimson weed—we cannot name them all. Rhubarb leaves, for example, either raw or cooked, can cause death or violent convulsions. Peach, elderberry, and cherry trees can cause cyanide poisoning if their bark is consumed.

There are also many insects that can be poisonous to dogs such as spiders, bees, wasps, and some flies. A few toads and frogs exude a fluid that can make a dog foam at the mouth—and even kill him—if he bites too hard!

There have been cases of dogs suffering nicotine poisoning by consuming the contents of full ashtrays which thoughtless smokers have left on the coffee table. Also, do not leave nails, staples, pins, or other sharp objects lying around. Likewise, don't let your puppy play with plastic bags which could suffocate him. Unplug, remove, or cover any electrical cords or wires near your dog. Chewing live wires could lead to severe mouth burns or death. Remember that an ounce of prevention is worth a pound of cure: keep all potentially dangerous objects out of your pet's reach.

Bufo marinus, *the giant toad, is a very large species of toad that, when provoked, will produce a secretion that is toxic if ingested. The giant toad can potentially be a canine killer.*

VEHICLE TRAVEL SAFETY

A dog should never be left alone in a car. It takes only a few minutes for the heat to become unbearable in the summer, and to drop to freezing in the winter.

A dog traveling in a car or truck should be well behaved. An undisciplined dog can be deadly in a moving vehicle. The dog should be trained to lie on the back seat of the vehicle. Allowing your dog to stick its head out of the window is unwise. The dog may jump or it may get something in its eye. Some manufacturers sell seat belts and car seats designed for dogs.

Traveling with your dog in the back of your pick-up truck is an unacceptable notion and dangerous to all involved.

PROTECT YOURSELF FIRST

In almost all first aid situations, the dog is in pain. He may indeed be in shock and not appear to be suffering, until you move him. Then he may bite your hand or resist being helped at all. So if you want to help your dog, help yourself first by tying his mouth closed. To do this, use a piece of strong cloth four inches wide and three feet long, depending on the size of the dog. Make a loop in the middle of the strip and slip it over his nose with the knot under his chin and over the bony part of his nose.

Pull it tight and bring the ends back around his head behind the ears and tie it tightly, ending with a bow knot for quick, easy release. Now you can handle the dog safely. As a dog perspires through his tongue, do not leave the "emergency muzzle" on any longer than necessary.

ADMINISTERING MEDICINE

When you are giving liquid medicine to your dog, it is a good idea to pull the lips away from the side of the mouth, form a lip pocket, and let the liquid trickle past the tongue. Remain at his side, never in front of the dog, as he may cough and spray you with the liquid. Moreover, you must never pour liquid medicine while the victim's tongue is drawn out, as inhalation pneumonia could be the disastrous result.

Medicine in pill form is best administered by forcing the dog's mouth open, holding his head back, and placing the capsule as far back on his tongue as you can reach. To do this: put the palm of your hand over the dog's muzzle (his foreface) with your fingers on one side of his jaw, your thumb

An injured dog can bite, rather unintentionally. A make-shift muzzle can be used in the case of an emergency. A tie or a torn piece of cloth can suffice.

To avoid inhalation pneumonia, a syringe placed between the dog's gums can be used when administering liquid medications.

on the other. Press his lips hard against his teeth while using your other hand to pull down his lower jaw. With your two fingers, try to put the pill as far back on the dog's tongue as you can reach. Keep his mouth and nostrils closed and he should be forced to swallow the medicine. As the dog will not be feeling well, stroke his neck to comfort him and to help him swallow his medicine more easily. Do keep an eye on him for a few moments afterward, however, to make certain that he does not spit it out.

IN CASE OF AN ACCIDENT

It is often difficult for you to assess the dog's injuries after a road accident. He may appear normal, but there might be internal hemorrhaging. A vital organ could be damaged or ribs broken. Keep the dog as quiet and warm as possible; cover him with blankets or your coat to let his own body heat build up. Signs of shock are a rapid and weak pulse, glassy-eyed appearance, subnormal temperature, and slow capillary refill time. To determine the last symptom, press firmly against the dog's gums until they turn white. Release and count the number of seconds until the gums return to their normal color. If it is more than 2–3 seconds, the dog may be going into shock. Failure to return to the reddish pink color indicates that the dog may be in serious trouble and needs immediate assistance.

If artificial respiration is required, first open the dog's mouth and check for obstructions; extend his tongue and examine the pharynx. Clear his mouth of mucus and blood and hold the mouth slightly open. Mouth-to-mouth resuscitation involves holding the dog's tongue to the bottom of his mouth with one hand and sealing his nostrils with the other while you blow into his mouth. Watch for his chest to rise with each inflation. Repeat every 5–6 seconds, the equivalent of 10–12 breaths a minute.

If the veterinarian cannot come to you, try to improvise a stretcher to take the dog to him.

To administer pills, simply press the dog's lips against his teeth until he opens his mouth. Then place the pill as far back on the tongue as possible. Now hold the dog's mouth closed and see that the dog has swallowed. Praise him for his cooperation.

To carry a puppy, wrap him in a blanket that has been folded into several thicknesses. If he is in shock, it is better to pick him up by holding one hand under his chest, the other under the hindquarters. This will keep him stretched out.

It is always better to roll an injured dog than to try and lift him. If you find him lying beside the road after a car accident, apply a muzzle even if you have to use someone's necktie to make one. Send someone for a blanket and roll him gently onto

Known as Elizabethan collars, these devices can be purchased at a pet store or provided by your veterinarian to prevent the dog from complications resulting from excessive licking or chewing.

it. Two people, one on each side, can make a stretcher out of the blanket and move the dog easily.

If no blanket is available and the injured dog must be moved, try to keep him as flat as possible. So many dogs' backs are broken in car accidents that one must first consider that possibility. However, if he can move his hind legs or tail, his spine is probably not broken. Get medical assistance for him immediately.

It should be mentioned that unfortunate car accidents, which can maim or kill your dog, can be avoided if he is confined at all times either indoors or, if out-of-doors, in a fenced-in yard or

Nightshade (left) *and larkspur* (right) *are two plants that are poisonous when ingested. Many dogs eat small amounts of wild grass, which is often harmless if not sprayed with pesticides; however, the owner must be cautious that poisonous plants are not growing in the grass, for they can be accidentally consumed.*

some other protective enclosure. *Never* allow your dog to roam free; even a well-trained dog may, for some unknown reason, dart into the street—and the result could be tragic.

If you need to walk your dog, leash him first so that he will be protected from moving vehicles.

PROTECTING YOUR PET

It is important to watch for any tell-tale signs of illness so that you can spare your pet any unnecessary suffering. Your dog's eyes, for example, should normally be bright and alert, so if the haw is bloodshot or partially covers the eye, it may be a sign of illness or irritation. If your dog has matter in the corners of his eyes, bathe them with a mild eye wash; obtain ointment or eye drops from your veterinarian to treat a chronic condition.

If your dog seems to have something wrong with his ears which causes him to scratch at them or shake his head, cautiously probe the ear with a cotton swab. An accumulation of wax will probably work itself out. Dirt or dried blood, however, is indicative of ear mites or infection and should be treated immediately. Sore ears in the summer, due to insect bites, should be washed with mild soap and water, then covered with a soothing ointment and wrapped in gauze if necessary. Keep your pet away from insects until his ears heal, even if this means confining him indoors.

INOCULATIONS

Periodic check-ups by your veterinarian throughout your puppy's life are good health insurance. The person from whom your puppy was purchased should tell you what inoculations your puppy has had and when the next visit to the vet is necessary. You must make certain that your puppy has been vaccinated against the following infectious canine diseases: distemper, canine hepatitis, leptospirosis, rabies, parvovirus, and parainfluenza. Annual "boosters" thereafter provide inexpensive protection for your dog against such serious diseases. Puppies should also be checked for worms at an early age.

DISTEMPER

Young dogs are most susceptible to distemper, although it may affect dogs of all ages. Some signs of the disease are loss of appetite, depression, chills, and fever, as well as a watery discharge from the eyes and nose. Unless treated promptly, the disease goes into advanced stages with infections of the lungs, intestines, and nervous system. Dogs that recover may be impaired with paralysis, convulsions, a twitch, or some other defect, usually spastic in nature. Early inoculations in puppyhood

While the vet is inspecting your dog, secure him around the base of his neck and the tuck of his abdomen.

When a dog's ear is injured, it should be bandaged by a professional. A protective collar should then be secured.

should be followed by an annual booster to help protect against this disease.

CANINE HEPATITIS

The signs of hepatitis are drowsiness, vomiting, loss of appetite, high temperature, and great thirst. These signs may be accompanied by swellings of the head, neck, and abdomen. Vomiting may also occur. This disease strikes quickly, and death may occur in only a few hours. An annual booster shot is needed after the initial series of puppy shots.

LEPTOSPIROSIS

Infection caused by either of two serovars, *canicola* or *copehageni* is usually begun by the dog's licking substances contaminated by the urine or feces of infected animals. Brown rats are the main carriers of *copehageni*. The signs are weakness, vomiting, and a yellowish discoloration of the jaws, teeth, and tongue, caused by an inflammation of the kidneys. A veterinarian can administer the bacterins to protect your dog from this disease. The frequency of the doses is determined by the risk factor involved.

RABIES

This disease of the dog's central nervous system spreads by infectious saliva, which is transmitted by the bite of an infected animal. Of the two main classes of signs, the first is "furious rabies," in which the dog shows a period of melancholy or depression, then irritation, and finally paralysis. The first period can be from a few hours to several days, and during this time the dog is cross and will change his position often, lose his appetite, begin to lick, and bite or swallow foreign objects. During this phase the dog is spasmodically wild and has impulses to run away. The dog acts fearless and bites everything in sight. If he is caged or confined, he will fight at the bars and possibly break teeth or fracture his jaw. His bark becomes a peculiar howl. In the final stage, the animal's lower jaw becomes paralyzed and hangs down. He then walks with a stagger, and saliva drips from his mouth. About four to eight days after the onset of paralysis, the dog dies.

The second class of symptoms is referred to as "dumb rabies" and is characterized by the dog's walking in a bearlike manner with his head down. The lower jaw is paralyzed and the dog is unable to bite. It appears as if he has a bone caught in his throat.

If a dog is bitten by a rabid animal, he probably can be saved if he is taken to a veterinarian in time for a series of injections. After the signs appear, however, no cure is possible. The local health

Rats are the carriers of many diseases, including leptospirosis.

department must be notified in the case of a rabid dog, for he is a danger to all who come near him. As with the other shots each year, an annual rabies inoculation is very important. In many areas, the administration of rabies vaccines for dogs is required by law.

PARVOVIRUS

This relatively new virus is a contagious disease that has spread in almost epidemic proportions throughout certain sections of the United States. It has also appeared in Australia, Canada, and Europe. Canine parvovirus attacks the intestinal tract, white blood cells, and heart muscle. It is believed to spread through dog-to-dog contact, and the specific course of infection seems to come from fecal matter of infected dogs. Overcoming parvovirus is difficult, for it is capable of existing in the environment for many months under varying conditions and temperatures, and it can be transmitted from place to place on the hair and feet of infected dogs, as well as on the clothes and shoes of people.

Vomiting and severe diarrhea, which will appear within five to seven days after the animal has been exposed to the virus, are the initial signs of this disease. At the onset of illness, feces will be light gray or yellow-gray in

It is believed that mice can carry the early-stage deer ticks that may be carriers of the dreaded lyme disease.

color, and the urine might be blood-streaked. Because of the vomiting and severe diarrhea, the dog that has contracted the disease will dehydrate quickly. Depression and loss of appetite, as well as a rise in temperature, can accompany the other symptoms. Death caused by this disease usually occurs within 48 to 72 hours following the appearance of the symptoms. Puppies are hardest hit, and the virus is fatal to 75 percent of puppies that contract it. Death in

Stable fly: a painful bite.

puppies can be within two days of the onset of the illness.

A series of shots administered by a veterinarian is the best preventive measure for canine parvovirus. It is also important to disinfect the area where the dog is housed by using one part sodium hypochlorite solution (household bleach) to thirty parts of water and to keep the dog from coming into contact with the fecal matter of other dogs.

Deer tick: a carrier of lyme.

LYME DISEASE

Known as a bacterial infection, Lyme disease is transmitted by ticks infected with a spirochete known as *Borrelia burgdorferi*. The disease is most often acquired by the parasitic bite of an infected deer tick, *Ixodes dammini*. While the range of symptoms is broad, common warning signs include: rash beginning at the bite and soon extending in a bullseye-targetlike fashion; chills, fever, lack of balance, lethargy, and stiffness; swelling and pain, especially in the joints, possibly leading to arthritis or arthritic conditions; heart problems, weak limbs, facial paralysis, and lack of tactile sensation. Although there is no known cure-all, tetracycline and some other drugs have been prescribed with various degrees of success. If you suspect that your dog has Lyme disease, contact your vet immediately.

PARAINFLUENZA

Parainfluenza, or infectious canine tracheobronchitis, is commonly known as "kennel cough." It is highly contagious, affects the upper respiratory system, and is spread through direct or indirect contact with already diseased dogs. It will readily infect dogs of all ages that have not been vaccinated or that were previously infected. While this condition is definitely one of the serious diseases in dogs, it is self-limiting, usually lasting only two to four weeks. The symptoms are high fever and intense, harsh coughing that brings up mucus. As long as your pet sees your veterinarian immediately, the chances for his complete recovery are excellent.

EXTERNAL PARASITES

A parasite is an animal that lives in or on an organism of another species, known as the host, without contributing to the well-being of the host. The majority of dogs' skin problems are parasitic in nature and an estimated 90% of puppies are born with parasites.

Ticks can cause serious problems to dogs where the latter have access to woods, fields, and vegetation in which large numbers of native mammals live. Ticks are usually found clinging to vegetation and attach themselves to animals

Deer fly: a welt-inducing bite.

passing by. They have eight legs and a heavy shield or shell-like covering on their upper surface. Only by keeping dogs away from tick-infested areas can ticks on dogs be prevented.

The flea is the single most common cause of skin and coat problems in dogs. There are 11,000 kinds of fleas which can transmit specific disorders like tapeworm and heartworm or transport smaller parasites onto your dog. The common tapeworm, for example, requires the flea as an intermediate host for completion of its life cycle.

A female flea can lay hundreds of eggs and these will become adults in less than three weeks. Depending on the temperature

Brown dog tick: a common parasite.

The bite of a single flea can cause an irritation that spreads quickly over the surface of the skin. For flea prevention, the dog and his living quarters should be treated regularly.

and the amount of moisture, large numbers of fleas can attack dogs. The ears of dogs, in particular, can play host to hundreds of fleas.

Fleas can lurk in crevices and cracks, carpets, and bedding for months, so frequent cleaning of your dog's environment is absolutely essential. If he is infected by other dogs, then have him bathed and "dipped," which means that he will be put into water containing a chemical that kills fleas. Your veterinarian will advise which dip to use, and your dog must be bathed for at least twenty minutes. These parasites are tenacious and remarkably agile creatures; fleas have existed since prehistoric times and have been found in arctic as well as tropical climates. Some experts claim that fleas can jump 150 times the length of their bodies; this makes them difficult to catch and kill. Thus, treating your pet for parasites without simultaneously

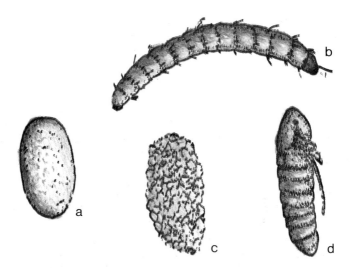

The life cycle of the flea: (a) egg (b) larvae (c) cocoon (d) pupae. If allowed to persist on the dog, fleas will build nests and reproduce, quickly infesting the dog. Regular brushing accompanied by anti-flea applications should suffice to eliminate the flea problem.

treating the environment is both inefficient and ineffective.

INTERNAL PARASITES

Four common internal parasites that may infect a dog are: roundworms, hookworms, whipworms, and tapeworms. The first three can be diagnosed by laboratory examination of the dog's stool, and tapeworms can be seen in the stool or attached to the hair around the anus. When a veterinarian determines what type of worm or worms are present, he then can advise the best treatment.

Roundworms, the dog's most common intestinal parasite, have a life cycle which permits complete eradication by worming twice, ten days apart. The first worming will remove all adults and the second will destroy all subsequently hatched eggs before they, in turn, can produce more parasites.

A dog in good physical condition is less susceptible to worm infestation than a weak dog. Proper sanitation and a nutritious diet help in preventing worms. One of the best preventive measures is to have clean, dry bedding for the dog, as this diminishes the possibility of reinfection due to flea or tick bites.

Heartworm infestation in dogs is passed by mosquitoes. Dogs with this disease tire easily, have difficulty in breathing, and lose weight despite a hearty appetite. Administration of preventive medicine throughout the spring, summer, and fall months is advised. A veterinarian must first take a blood sample from the dog to test for the presence of the disease, and if the dog is heartworm-free, pills or liquid medicine can be prescribed.

Heartworm life cycle: a carrier mosquito bites a dog and deposits microfilariae; the filariae travel through the dog's blood stream, lodging in the heart to reproduce. The carrier dog is later bitten by an uninfected mosquito, which thereby acquires uninfectious microfilariae, develops the microfilariae to an infectious stage, bites and infects another dog.

CANINE SENIOR CITIZENS

The processes of aging and gradual degenerative changes start far earlier in a dog than often observed, usually at about seven years of age. If we recall that each year of a dog's life roughly corresponds to about seven years in the life of a man, by the age of seven he is well into middle age. Your pet will become less active, will have a poorer appetite with increased thirst, there will be frequent periods of constipation and less than normal passage of urine. His skin and coat might become dull and dry and his hair will become thin and fall out. There is a tendency towards obesity in old age, which should be avoided by maintaining a regular exercise program. Remember, also, that your pet will be less able to cope

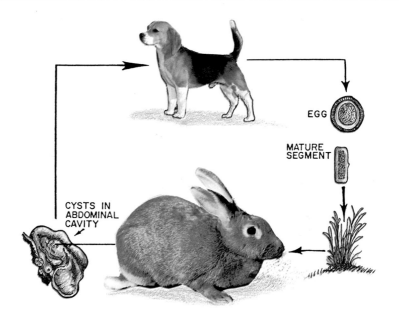

EGG

MATURE SEGMENT

CYSTS IN
ABDOMINAL
CAVITY

Tapeworms can be acquired in a number of ways; the infected dog must receive veterinary treatment.

with extreme heat, cold, fatigue, and change in routine.

There is the possibility of loss or impairment of hearing or eyesight. He may become bad-tempered more often than in the past. Other ailments such as rheumatism, arthritis, kidney infections, heart disease, male prostatism, and hip dysplasia may occur. Of course, all these require a veterinarian's examination and recommendation of suitable treatment. Care of the teeth is also important in the aging dog.

Indeed, the mouth can be a barometer of nutritional health. Degenerating gums, heavy tartar on the teeth, loose teeth, and sore lips are common. The worst of all diseases in old age, however, is neglect. Good care in early life will have its effect on your dog's later years; the nutrition and general health care of his first few years can determine his lifespan and the quality of his life. It is worth bearing in mind that the older, compared to the younger, animal needs more protein of good biological value, more vitamins A, B-complex, D and E, more calcium and iron, less fat and fewer carbohydrates.

Preventive Dental Care

ALL DOGS NEED TO CHEW

Puppies and young dogs need something with resistance to chew on while their teeth and jaws are developing—to cut the puppy teeth, to induce growth of the permanent teeth under the puppy teeth, to assist in getting rid of the puppy teeth on time, to help the permanent teeth through the gums, to assure normal jaw development and to settle the permanent teeth solidly in the jaws.

The adult dog's desire to chew stems from the instinct for tooth cleaning, gum massage, and jaw exercise—plus the need to vent periodic doggie tensions. . . . A pacifier if you will!

Dental caries, as they affect the teeth of humans, are virtually

It is imperative that the owner take the necessary measures to ensure sound dental health. Ideal canine dentition illustrated: upper palate on right; lower palate on left.

unknown in dogs; but tartar (calculus) accumulates on the teeth of dogs, particularly at the gum line, more rapidly than on the teeth of humans. These accumulations, if not removed, bring irritation and then infection, which erode the tooth enamel and ultimately destroy the teeth at the roots. It is important that you take your dog to your local veterinarian for periodic dental examinations.

Tooth and jaw development will normally continue until the dog is more than a year old—but sometimes much longer, depending upon the dog, its chewing exercise, rate of calcium utilization and many other factors, known and unknown, which affect the development of individual dogs. Diseases, like distemper for example, may sometimes arrest development of the teeth and jaws, which may resume months or even years later.

This is why dogs, especially puppies and young dogs, will often destroy valuable property when their chewing instinct is not diverted from their owners'

his instinct tells him to chew. If your purposes, and those of your dog, are to be accomplished, what you provide for chewing must be desirable from the doggie viewpoint, have the necessary functional qualities, and, above all, be safe.

It is very important that dogs be prohibited from chewing on anything they can break or indigestible things from which they can bite sizeable chunks. Sharp pieces, such as those from a bone which can be broken by a dog, may pierce the intestinal wall and kill.

possessions, particularly during the widely varying critical period for young dogs. Saving your possessions from destruction, assuring proper development of teeth and jaws, providing for "interim" tooth cleaning and gum massage, and channeling doggie tensions into a non-destructive outlet are, therefore, all dependent upon the dog's having something suitable for chewing readily available when

A dog's teeth with little to no calculus build-up, a state achievable through consistent and appropriate care.

Indigestible things which can be bitten off in chunks, such as toys made of rubber compound or cheap plastic, may cause an intestinal stoppage; if not regurgitated, they are certain to bring painful death unless surgery is promptly performed.

NATURAL CHEW BONES

Strong natural bones, such as 4- to 8-inch lengths of round shin bone from mature beef—either the kind you can get from your butcher or one of the varieties available commercially in pet stores—may serve your dog's teething needs, if his mouth is large enough to handle them.

You may be tempted to give your puppy a smaller bone and he may not be able to break it when you do, but puppies grow rapidly and the power of their jaws constantly increases until maturity. This means that a growing dog may break one of the smaller bones at any time, swallow the pieces and die painfully before you realize what is wrong.

Many people have the mistaken notion that their dog's teeth are like those of wild carnivores or of dogs from antiquity. The teeth of wild carnivorous animals and those found in the fossils of the dog-like creatures of antiquity have far thicker and stronger enamel than those of our dogs today.

All hard natural bones are highly abrasive. If your dog is an avid chewer, natural bones may wear away his teeth prematurely; hence, they then should be taken away from your dog when the teething purposes have been served. The badly worn, and usually painful, teeth of many mature dogs can be traced to excessive chewing on animal bones. Contrary to popular belief, knuckle bones that can be chewed up and swallowed by the dog provide little, if any, useable calcium or other nutrient. They do, however, disturb the digestion of most dogs and might cause them to vomit the nourishing food they really need.

Never give a dog your old shoe to chew on, even if you have removed all the nails or metal parts, such as lace grommets, buckles, metal arches, and so on. Rubber heels are especially dangerous, as the dog can bite off chunks, swallow them, and suffer from intestinal blockage as a result. Additionally, if the rubber should happen to have a nail imbedded in it that you cannot detect, this could pierce or tear the intestinal wall. There is always the possibility, too, that your dog may fail to differentiate between his shoe and yours and chew up a good pair while you're not looking. It is strongly recommended that you refrain from offering old shoes as chew toys, since there are much safer products available.

RAWHIDE CHEWS

The most popular material from which dog chews are made is the hide from cows, horses, and other animals. Most of these chews are made in foreign countries where the quality of the hide is not good enough for

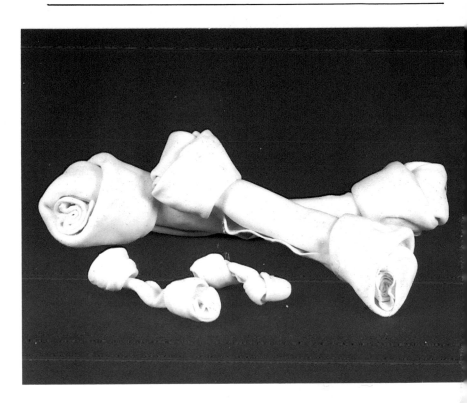

Many dogs love rawhide, and many stores carry a variety of rawhide chew products.

making leather. These foreign hides may contain lead, antibiotics, arsenic, or insecticides which might be detrimental to the health of your dog . . . or even your children. It is not impossible that a small child will start chewing on a piece of rawhide meant for the dog! Rawhide chews do not serve the primary chewing functions very well. They are also a bit messy when wet from mouthing, and most dogs chew them up rather rapidly. They have been considered safe for dogs until recently.

Rawhide is flavorful to dogs. They like it. Currently, some veterinarians have been attributing cases of acute constipation to large pieces of incompletely digested rawhide in the intestine. Basically it is good for them to chew on, but dogs think rawhide is food. They do not play with it nor do they use it as a pacifier to relieve doggie tension. They eat it as they would any other food. This is dangerous, for the hide is very difficult for dogs to digest and swallow, and many dogs choke on large particles of rawhide that become stuck in their throats. *Before you offer your dog rawhide chews, consult your veterinarian.* Vets have a lot of

Annealed nylon chews are recommended by veterinarians as proven-safe and effective canine chew devices.

experience with canine chewing devices; ask them what they recommend.

NYLON CHEW DEVICES

The nylon bones, especially those with natural meat and bone flavor added, are probably the most complete, safe, and economical answer to the chewing need. Dogs cannot break them nor bite off sizeable chunks; hence, they are completely safe. And being longer lasting than other things offered for the purpose, they are very economical.

Hard chewing raises little bristle-like projections on the surface of the nylon bones to provide effective interim tooth cleaning and vigorous gum massage, much in the same way your toothbrush does it for you. The little projections are raked off and swallowed in the form of thin shavings, but the chemistry of the nylon is such that they break down in the stomach fluids and pass through without effect.

The toughness of the nylon provides the strong chewing resistance needed for important jaw exercise and effective help for the teething functions; however, there is no tooth wear because nylon is non-abrasive. Being inert, nylon does not support the growth of microorganisms, and it can be washed in soap and water or sterilized by boiling or in an autoclave.

There are a great variety of Nylabone® products available that veterinarians recommend as safe and healthy for your dog or puppy to chew on. These Nylabone® Pooch Pacifiers® usually don't splinter, chip, or break off in large chunks; instead, they are frizzled by the

One of the many advantages of annealed nylon chew products is durability and long life. To keep your Nylabone® products sterile and to re-energize their flavor, these bones can be boiled in broth.

dog's chewing action, and this creates a toothbrush-like surface that cleanses the teeth and massages the gums. At the same time, these hard-nylon therapeutic devices channel doggie tension and chewing frustation into constructive rather than destructive behavior. The original nylon bone (Nylabone®) is not a toy and dogs use it only when in need of pacification. Keeping a bone in each of your dog's recreation rooms is the best method of providing the requisite pacification. Unfortunately, many nylon chew products have been copied. These inferior quality copies are sold in supermarkets and other chain stores. The really good products are sold only through veterinarians, pet shops, grooming salons and places where the sales people really know something about dogs. The good products have the flavor impregnated *into* the bone. This makes the taste last longer. The smell is undetectable to humans. The artificial bones which have a strong odor are poor-quality bones with the odor sprayed on to impress the dog owner (not the dog)! These heavily scented dog toys may impart the odor to your carpets or furniture if an odor-sprayed bone lies there wet from a dog's chewing on it.

Food particles can be deposited between the teeth, where they are difficult to remove. Even the best chew products may not be able to free these decaying food pieces. For this reason, the Nylafloss® dental device is recommended. It is the only effective product to clean between the dog's teeth.

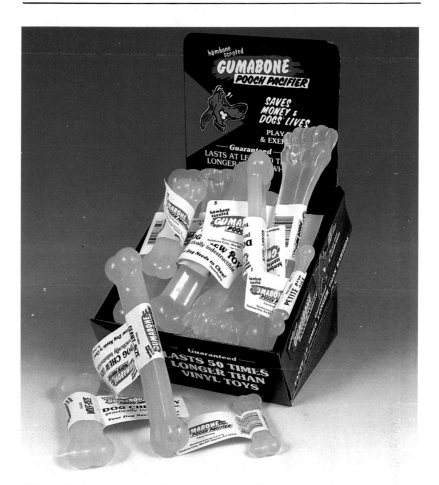

While satisfying the deep-rooted desire to chew, the dog's chewing a Gumabone® works to prevent tartar and plaque build-up. A dog should have access to an effective chew product at all times.

FLOSS OR LOSS!

Most dentists relay that brushing daily is just not enough. In order to prevent unnecessary tooth loss, flossing is essential. For dogs, human dental floss is not the answer—however, canine dental devices are available. The Nylafloss® is a revolutionary product that is designed to save dogs teeth and keep them healthy. Even though your dogs won't believe you, Nylafloss® is not a toy but rather

Prevention is the key to good dental health. It makes little sense to ignore your dog's dental needs; tooth problems can be costly and detrimental to your dog's well being. Nylafloss® is one very important part of preventive dental care.

a most effective agent in removing destructive plaque between the teeth and *beneath* the gum line where gum disease begins. Gentle tugging is all that is necessary to activate the Nylafloss®. These 100% inert nylon products are guaranteed to outlast rawhide chews by ten times and are available for sale at all pet shops.

THE IMPORTANCE OF PREVENTION

In order to get to the root of canine dentistry problems, it is important for owners to realize that no less than 75% of all canine dental health problems serious enough to require a vet's assistance and nearly 98% of all canine teeth lost are attributable to periodontal disease. Periodontal disease not only mars the teeth but also the gums and other buccal tissue in the mouth. Severe cases of periodontal disease involve resultant bacterial toxins which are absorbed into the blood stream and cause permanent damage to the heart and kidneys. In the infected mouth, teeth are loosened; tartar, unsightly and bad smelling, accumulates heavily; and the dog experiences a complete loss of appetite. Long-standing periodontitis can also manifest itself in simple symptoms such as diarrhea and vomiting.

Periodontal disease deserves the attention of every dog owner—a dog's teeth are extremely important to his ongoing health. The accumulation of plaque, food matter mixed with saliva attaching itself to the tooth surface, is a sure sign of potential bacteria build-up. As toxic material gathers, the bone surrounding the teeth erodes. If plaque and calculus continue to reside without attention, bacteria-fighting cells will form residual pus at the root of the teeth, dividing the gum from the tooth. The debris is toxic and actually kills the buccal tissue. This is a most undesirable situation, as hardened dental calculus is one of the most direct causative agents of periodontitis.

In actuality, the disease is a result of a number of contributing factors. Old age, a diet comprised solely of soft or semi-soft foods, dental tartar, constant chewing of hair and even coprophagy (the eating of stool) are among the most common contributors.

Just as regular dental visits and brushing are necessary for humans, regular hygienic care and veterinary check-ups can help control tooth problems in canines. Involved and expensive routines can be performed on the affected, neglected mouth and teeth if decay has begun

eroding the enamel and infecting the gums. Cleaning, polishing, and scaling are routine to remove calculus build-up.

Owners must claim responsibility for their dog's health, and tooth care is no small aspect of the care required. Daily brushing with a salt/baking soda solution is the best answer, but many owners find this tedious or just too difficult to perform. The simpler and more proven effective way to avoid, reduce, and fight periodontal disease and calculus build-up is giving the dog regular access to a thermoplastic polymer chew device. The Gumabone® products are the only scientifically proven line that offers the desired protection from calculus and tartar build-up.

CANINE DENTAL BREAKTHROUGH

The independent research of Dr. Andrew Duke, D.V.M., reveals that 70% of the dogs that regularly use Gumabone® experience a reduction of calculus build-up. This find is a breakthrough for the dog world, since the Gumabone® has already resided in the toy boxes of many dogs as their favorite play item. Little did owners know previously that their dogs were gaining entertainment and unparalleled dental treatment at the same time. Dr. Duke writes: "There is little debate left that

THE CALCULUS INDEX

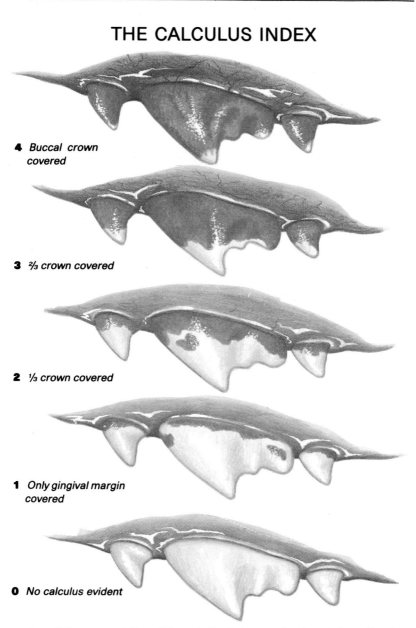

4 *Buccal crown covered*

3 *⅔ crown covered*

2 *⅓ crown covered*

1 *Only gingival margin covered*

0 *No calculus evident*

*An artist's representation of the calculus index, ranging from index rating **4** (topmost drawing) through index rating **0** (lowest drawing).*

dental calculus is an excellent indicator of periodontal health in the dog, just as it is in humans. "Calculus does not cause gingivitis and periodontitis, but the plaque and bacteria that cause periodontitis are responsible for the mineral precipitation we know as 'calculus.' All veterinarians who have made a study of dogs' oral

A dog's teeth showing a moderate calculus build-up.

health have noticed the middle aged dog who actively chews with excellent gingival health. Many of these dogs that chew hard substances regularly wear the cusps down and even may expose the pulp cavity faster than secondary dentin can be formed. Often these 'excellent chewers' are presented with slab fractures of the premolars or apical abcesses.

"The challenge then becomes to find a substance which is effective in removing calculus and plaque but does not wear the enamel excessively. In an attempt to duplicate the chewstuffs enjoyed by dogs in the wild, researchers have used bovine tracheas to demonstrate the inhibition of plaque and gingivitis. Very little else has been done in veterinary medicine to establish a scientific basis for evaluating chewstuffs.

"In the human field it is generally accepted (incorrectly) that fibrous foodstuffs and diet have no effect on oral health. This is a moot point since the practice of brushing is by far a more efficient technique of preventing plaque accumulation, calculus and periodontal disease. Studies in human subjects failed to find any benefits in eating apples, raw carrots, etc. If people are not allowed to brush, it is difficult to conduct clinical trials of more than one week.

"The increased awareness of animals' dental health of recent years has resulted in most veterinary practitioners' recommending some kind of chewstuff to their dog owners. To meet this market demand, there has been a stampede into the market by vendors ready to promote their products. The veterinarian is furnished no

Plaque is formed by the food debris and bacterial deposits on the teeth. Due to the high carbon dioxide and pH level in the mouth, minerals precipitate on the plaque to form calculus.

scientific data, but is asked to promote rawhide, bounce, and squeaky toys. How would our human colleagues handle this situation? Can Listerine® say that it prevents colds, but not support the claim? Can Tartar Control Crest® or Colgate Tartar Control Formula® be sold if it is not proven that it does in fact reduce tartar? Of course not.

"To this end, the following study was made.

"*Method:* Twenty dogs of different breeds and age were selected from a veterinary practice's clientele. Although most were from multiple pet households, none were colony dogs. The owners were asked if they would allow their dogs to be anesthetized for two prophylactic cleanings which included root planing, polishing, and gingival debridement necessary to insure good oral hygiene.

"The dogs were divided into two groups of 10. Their teeth were cleaned and their calculus index converted to 0. One group was allowed only their normal dry commercial dog ration for 30 days. The other was allowed to have free choice access to Gumabone® products of the appropriate size.

"After 30 days, photoslides were made of the upper 3rd premolar, upper 4th premolar, and the lower 4th premolar on both sides of the dog's mouth. The dogs were again subjected to a prophylactic cleaning and the group reversed. After the second 30 days, photoslides were again made. A total of six teeth in each mouth were evaluated on each dog. This was 80 slides representing 240 teeth."

Fourteen out of 20 dogs (or 70%) experienced a reduction in calculus build-up by regularly

Regular use of the Gumabone® chew products can significantly reduce plaque build-up.

using the Gumabone® product. These products are available in a variety of sizes (for different size dogs) and designed in interesting shapes: bones, balls, knots and rings (and even a tug toy). The entertainment value of the Gumabone® products is but an added advantage to the fighting of tooth decay and periodontitis. The products are ham-flavored and made of a thermoplastic polymer that is designed to outlast by ten times any other rawhide, rubber or vinyl chew product, none of which can promise the proven benefit of the Gumabone®.

If your dog is able to chew apart a Gumabone®, it is probable that you provided him with a bone that is too small for him. Replace it with a larger one and the problem should not re-

Teeth of affected canine showing little to no plaque or calculus build-up after professional cleaning.

Above: The clean healthy teeth that are desired in dogs should inspire owners to work towards better dental hygiene. *Below:* The beginning of undesirable deposits forming on improperly maintained teeth.

materialize. Economically, the Gumabone® is a smart choice, even without comparing it to the cost of extensive dental care.

Of course, nothing can *substitute* for periodic professional attention to your dog's teeth and gums, no more than your toothbrush can replace your dentist. Have your dog's teeth cleaned by your veterinarian at least once a year—twice a year is better—and he will be healthier, happier, and a far more pleasant companion.

Gumabones® are available through veterinarians and pet shops.

Breeding

If you own a bitch and you want to breed her, first make sure you can handle the responsibility of caring for her and her litter of pups. Consider the time and money involved just to get her into breeding condition and then to sustain her throughout pregnancy and afterwards while she tends her young. You will be obligated to house, feed, groom, and housebreak the puppies until good homes can be found for them; and, lest we forget, there will be periodic trips to the vet for check-ups, wormings, and inoculations. Common sense should tell you that it is indeed cruel to bring unwanted or unplanned puppies into an already crowded canine world; only negligent pet owners allow this to happen. With pet-quality purebred dogs, most breeders require prospective pet owners to sign a neuter/spay agreement when they purchase their dogs. In this way breeders can be assured that only their very best stock of show-quality and breeder-quality animals, i.e., those that match closely their individual standards of perfection and those that are free of genetic disorders or disease, will be used to propagate the breed.

Before you select a stud to mate with your bitch, think carefully about why you want her to give birth to a litter of puppies. If you feel she will be deprived in some way if she is not bred, if you think your children will learn from the experience, if you have the mistaken notion that you will make money from this great undertaking, think again. A dog can lead a perfectly happy, healthy, normal life without having been mated; in fact, spaying a female and neutering a male helps them become better pets, as they are not so anxious to search for a mate in an effort to relieve their sexual tensions. As for giving the children a lesson in sex education, this is hardly a valid reason for breeding your dog. And on an economic level, it takes not only years of hard work (researching pedigrees and bloodlines, studying genetics, among other things), but it takes plenty of capital (money, equipment, facilities) to make a decent profit from dog breeding. Why most dedicated breeders are lucky just to break even. If you have only a casual interest in dog breeding, it is best to leave this pastime to those who are more experienced in such matters, those who consider it a serious hobby or vocation. If you have bought a breeder– or show-quality canine, one that may be capable of producing champions, and if you are just starting out with this breeding venture, seek advice from the seller of your dog, from other veteran breeders, and from your vet before you begin.

Breeding

THE FEMALE "IN SEASON"

A bitch may come into season (also known as "heat" or estrus) once or several times a year, depending on the particular breed and the individual dog. Her first seasonal period, that is to say, the time when she is capable of being fertilized by a male dog, may occur as early as six months with some breeds. If you own a female and your portion of the female's reproductive tract; the soft, flabby vulva indicates her readiness to mate. Around this second week or so ovulation occurs, and this is the crucial period for her to be bred, if this is what you have in mind for her. It is during this middle phase of the heat cycle when conception can take place. Just remember that there is great variation from

intention is *not* to breed her, by all means discuss with the vet the possibility of having her spayed: this means before she reaches sexual maturity.

The first sign of the female's being in season is a thin red discharge, which may increase for about a week; it then changes color to a thin yellowish stain, which lasts about another week. Simultaneously, there is a swelling of the vulva, the exterior

Cells reproduce by a process called mitosis, in which the cells divide, forming two identical cells.

bitch to bitch with regard to how often they come into heat, how long the heat cycles last, how long the period of ovulation lasts, and how much time elapses between heat cycles. Generally, after the third week of heat, the vulval swelling decreases and the estrus period

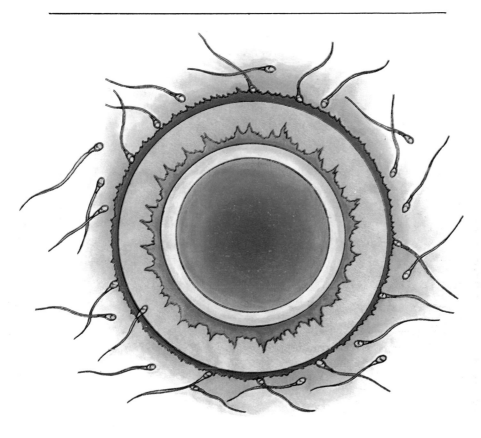

ceases for several months.

It should be mentioned that the female will probably lose her puppy coat, or at least shed part of it, about three months after she has come into season. This is the time when her puppies would have been weaned, had she been mated, and females generally drop coat at this time.

With female dogs, there are few, if any, behavioral changes during estrus. A bitch may dart out of an open door to greet all

The egg within the female is surrounded by a wall that normally takes many sperm to penetrate. In this way, only the strongest sperm will fertilize the egg. A fertile female in season usually has a number of eggs, known as gametes.

available male dogs that show an interest in her, and she may occasionally raise her tail and assume a mating stance, particularly if you pet her lower back; but these signs are not as dramatic as those of the sexually mature male. He himself does not experience heat cycles; rather, he is attracted to the female during all phases of her seasonal period. He usually becomes more aggressive and tends to fight with other males, especially over females in heat. He tends to mark his territory with urine to attract females and at the same time to warn other competitive males. It is not uncommon to see him mount various objects, and people, in an effort to satisfy his mature sexual urges.

If you are a homeowner and you have an absolutely climb-proof and dig-proof run within your yard, it may be safe to leave your bitch in season there. But then again it may not be a wise idea, as there have been cases of males mating with females right through chain-link fencing! Just to be on the safe side, shut her indoors during her heat periods and don't let her outdoors until you are certain the estrus period is over. Never leave a bitch in heat outdoors, unsupervised, even for a minute so that she can defecate or

A whelping box provides the female with a safe place to deliver her pups. Introduce the female to the box several days prior to delivery to get her adjusted to it. Later, when whelping is near, move her to the box so that she may prepare for delivery.

urinate. If you want to prevent the neighborhood dogs from hanging around your doorstep, as they inevitably will do when they discover your female is in season, take her some distance away from the house before you let her do her business. Otherwise, these canine suitors will be attracted to her by the arousing odor of her urine, and they will know instinctively that she isn't far from her scented

While in the womb, each pup is encased within a protective sac.

"calling card." If you need to walk your bitch, take her in the car to a nearby park or field for a chance to stretch her legs. Remember that after about three weeks, and this varies from dog to dog, you can let her outdoors again with no worry that she can have puppies until the next heat period.

Breeding

WHEN TO BREED

It is usually best to breed a bitch when she comes into her second or third season. Plan in advance the time of year which is best for you, taking into account your own schedule of activities (vacations, business trips, social engagements, and so on). Make sure you will be able to set aside plenty of time to assist with whelping of the newborn pups and caring for the dam and her litter for the next few weeks. At the very least, it probably will take an hour or so each day just to feed and clean up after the brood—but undoubtedly you will find it takes much longer if you stop to admire and play with the youngsters periodically! Refrain from selling the litter until it is at least six weeks old, keeping in mind that a litter of pups takes up a fair amount of space by then. It will be your responsibility to provide for them until they have been weaned from their mother, properly socialized, housebroken, and ready to go to new homes (unless you plan to keep them all). Hopefully, as strongly recommended, you will have already lined up buyers for the pups in advance of their arrival into this world.

CHOOSING THE STUD

You can plan to breed your female about six-and-one-half months after the start of her last season, although a variation of a month or two either way is not unusual. Do some research into the various bloodlines within your breed and then choose a stud dog and make arrangements well in advance. If you are breeding for show stock, which will command higher prices than pet-quality animals, a mate should be chosen very carefully. He should complement any deficiencies (bad traits) that your female may have, and he should have a good show record or be the sire of show winners, if he is old enough to have proven himself. If possible, the bitch and stud should have several ancestors in common within the last two or three generations, as such combinations have been known, generally, to "click" best.

The owner of a stud dog usually charges a stud fee for use of the animal's services. This does not always guarantee a litter, but if she fails to conceive, chances are you may be able to breed your female to that stud

Facing page: Dogs have an average gestation period of 63 to 65 days. This chart gives the expected delivery date according to the date on which the bitch was mated. The due date is an approximation only, and the owner should be prepared well in advance of the due date, especially with first-time mothers. If a bitch is mated more than once, the owner should use the date of the first mating but realize the possibility of a later delivery.

PERPETUAL WHELPING CHART

Bred / Due	1	2	3	4	5	6	7	8	9	10	11	12	13	14	15	16	17	18	19	20	21	22	23	24	25	26	27	28	29	30	31
Bred—Jan.	1	2	3	4	5	6	7	8	9	10	11	12	13	14	15	16	17	18	19	20	21	22	23	24	25	26	27	28	29	30	31
Due—March	5	6	7	8	9	10	11	12	13	14	15	16	17	18	19	20	21	22	23	24	25	26	27	28	29	30	31	April 1	2	3	4
Bred—Feb.	1	2	3	4	5	6	7	8	9	10	11	12	13	14	15	16	17	18	19	20	21	22	23	24	25	26	27	28			
Due—April	5	6	7	8	9	10	11	12	13	14	15	16	17	18	19	20	21	22	23	24	25	26	27	28	29	30	May 1	2			
Bred—Mar.	1	2	3	4	5	6	7	8	9	10	11	12	13	14	15	16	17	18	19	20	21	22	23	24	25	26	27	28	29	30	31
Due—May	3	4	5	6	7	8	9	10	11	12	13	14	15	16	17	18	19	20	21	22	23	24	25	26	27	28	29	30	31	June 1	2
Bred—Apr.	1	2	3	4	5	6	7	8	9	10	11	12	13	14	15	16	17	18	19	20	21	22	23	24	25	26	27	28	29	30	
Due—June	3	4	5	6	7	8	9	10	11	12	13	14	15	16	17	18	19	20	21	22	23	24	25	26	27	28	29	30	July 1	2	
Bred—May	1	2	3	4	5	6	7	8	9	10	11	12	13	14	15	16	17	18	19	20	21	22	23	24	25	26	27	28	29	30	31
Due—July	3	4	5	6	7	8	9	10	11	12	13	14	15	16	17	18	19	20	21	22	23	24	25	26	27	28	29	30	31	August 1	2
Bred—June	1	2	3	4	5	6	7	8	9	10	11	12	13	14	15	16	17	18	19	20	21	22	23	24	25	26	27	28	29	30	
Due—August	3	4	5	6	7	8	9	10	11	12	13	14	15	16	17	18	19	20	21	22	23	24	25	26	27	28	29	30	31	Sept. 1	
Bred—July	1	2	3	4	5	6	7	8	9	10	11	12	13	14	15	16	17	18	19	20	21	22	23	24	25	26	27	28	29	30	31
Due—September	2	3	4	5	6	7	8	9	10	11	12	13	14	15	16	17	18	19	20	21	22	23	24	25	26	27	28	29	30	Oct. 1	2
Bred—Aug.	1	2	3	4	5	6	7	8	9	10	11	12	13	14	15	16	17	18	19	20	21	22	23	24	25	26	27	28	29	30	31
Due—October	3	4	5	6	7	8	9	10	11	12	13	14	15	16	17	18	19	20	21	22	23	24	25	26	27	28	29	30	31	Nov. 1	2
Bred—Sept.	1	2	3	4	5	6	7	8	9	10	11	12	13	14	15	16	17	18	19	20	21	22	23	24	25	26	27	28	29	30	
Due—November	3	4	5	6	7	8	9	10	11	12	13	14	15	16	17	18	19	20	21	22	23	24	25	26	27	28	29	30	Dec. 1	2	
Bred—Oct.	1	2	3	4	5	6	7	8	9	10	11	12	13	14	15	16	17	18	19	20	21	22	23	24	25	26	27	28	29	30	31
Due—December	3	4	5	6	7	8	9	10	11	12	13	14	15	16	17	18	19	20	21	22	23	24	25	26	27	28	29	30	31	Jan. 1	2
Bred—Nov.	1	2	3	4	5	6	7	8	9	10	11	12	13	14	15	16	17	18	19	20	21	22	23	24	25	26	27	28	29	30	
Due—January	3	4	5	6	7	8	9	10	11	12	13	14	15	16	17	18	19	20	21	22	23	24	25	26	27	28	29	30	31	Feb. 1	
Bred—Dec.	1	2	3	4	5	6	7	8	9	10	11	12	13	14	15	16	17	18	19	20	21	22	23	24	25	26	27	28	29	30	31
Due—February	2	3	4	5	6	7	8	9	10	11	12	13	14	15	16	17	18	19	20	21	22	23	24	25	26	27	28	March 1	2	3	4

again. In some instances the owner of the stud will agree to take a "first pick of the litter" in place of a fee. You should, of course, settle all details beforehand, including the possibility of a single puppy surviving, deciding the age at which the pup is to be taken, and so forth.

If you plan to raise a litter that will be sold exclusively as pets,

The reproductive system of the female dog consists of a highly specialized group of organs situated at the rear of the animal.

and if you merely plan to make use of an available male (not a top stud dog), the most important selection point involves temperament. Make sure the dog is friendly, as well as healthy, because a bad disposition can be passed on to his puppies—and this is the worst of all traits in a dog destined to be a pet. If you are breeding pet-quality dogs, a "stud fee puppy," not necessarily the choice of the litter, is the usual payment. Don't

Ext. iliac a. & v.

R. uterine horn

Ovary

Wing of sacrum

Postcava

Colon

Vagina

Bladder

Reproductive organs in the bitch. Ext. = external; a. = artery; v. = vein; R. = right.

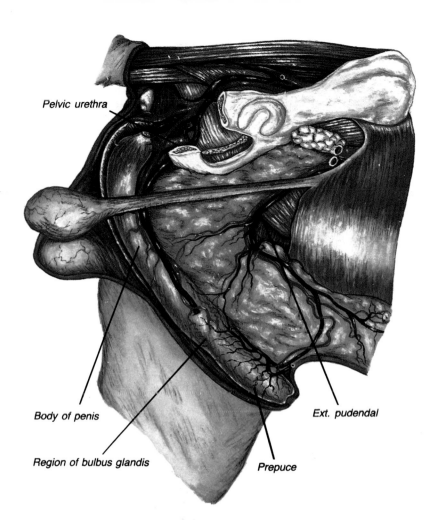

Pelvic urethra

Body of penis

Region of bulbus glandis

Ext. pudendal

Prepuce

The reproductive system of the male dog includes the penis and testicles. The sperm and testosterone producing testes are contained within the scrotal sac. When not excited, the penis is withdrawn into the dog. The dog's penis is unique in that the base of the shaft has a bulbous swelling that forbids retraction from the vagina until some time has passed after intercourse.

breed indiscriminately; be sure you will be able to find good homes for each of the pups, or be sure you have the facilities to keep them yourself, *before* you plan to mate your dog.

PREPARATION FOR BREEDING

Before you breed your female, make sure she is in good health.

Breeding

She should be neither too thin nor too fat. Any skin disease *must* be cured first so that it is not passed on to the puppies. If she has worms, she should be wormed before being bred or within three weeks after the mating. It is generally considered a good idea to revaccinate her against distemper and hepatitis before the puppies are born. This will increase the immunity the puppies receive during their early, most vulnerable period.

The female will probably be ready to breed twelve days after the first colored discharge appears. You can usually make arrangements to board her with the owner of the stud for a few days, to insure her being there at the proper time; or you can take her to be mated and bring her home the same day if you live near enough to the stud's owner. If the bitch still appears receptive she may be bred again two days later, just to make certain the mating was successful. However, some females never show signs of willingness, so it helps to have an experienced breeder on hand. In fact, you both may have to assist with the

The canine uterus is quite different from the human uterus. Besides the difference in shape, the canine uterus is designed to house an average of five to eight offspring.

OVARY

HORN OF UTERUS

BLADDER

BODY OF UTERUS

CANINE UTERUS
Before mating

VAGINA

OVARY →

HORN OF UTERUS →

WHELP →

BODY OF UTERUS →

VAGINA →

CANINE UTERUS
With Whelps

Prior to birth, the developing pups are housed in the horns of the uterus.

mating by holding the animals against each other to ensure the "tie" is not broken, that is, to make certain copulation takes place. Sometimes, too, you'll need to muzzle the bitch to keep her from biting you or the stud.

Usually the second day after the discharge changes color is the proper time to mate the bitch, and she may be bred for about three days following this time. For an additional week or so, she may have some discharge and attract other dogs by her odor; but she should not be bred. Once she has been bred, keep her far from all other

male dogs, as they have the capacity to impregnate her again and sire some of her puppies. This could prove disastrous where purebred puppies— especially show-quality ones— are concerned.

THE FEMALE IN WHELP

You can expect the puppies nine weeks from the day of the mating, although sixty-one days is as common as sixty-three. Gestation, that period when the pups are developing inside their mother, varies among individual bitches. During this time the female should receive normal care and exercise. If she was overweight at the start, don't increase her food right away; excess weight at whelping time can be a problem with some dogs. If she is on the thin side, however, supplement her meal or meals with a portion of milk and biscuit at noontime. This will help build her up and put weight on her.

You may want to add a mineral and vitamin supplement to her diet, on the advice of your veterinarian, since she will need an extra supply not only for herself but for the puppies growing inside of her. As the mother's appetite increases, feed her more. During the last two weeks of pregnancy, the pups grow enormously and the mother will have little room for food and less of an appetite. She should be tempted with meat, liver, and milk, however.

As the female in whelp grows heavier, cut out violent exercise

Using simple genetic rules, an owner can predict to some degree the traits that the offspring of a given mating can exhibit. The six possible ways in which a pair of determiners can unite are illustrated on this Mendelian expectation chart. Ratios apply to expectancy over large numbers, except in lines 1, 2, and 6 where exact expectancy is realized in every litter.

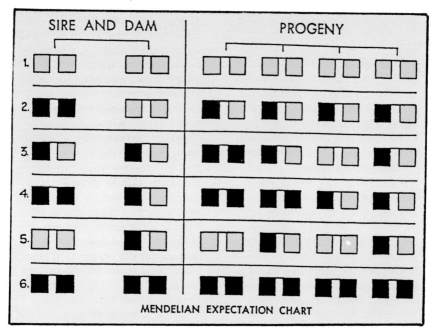

MENDELIAN EXPECTATION CHART

and jumping from her usual routine. Although a dog used to such activities will often play with the children or run around voluntarily, restrain her for her own sake.

A sign that whelping is imminent is the loss of hair around her breasts. This is nature's way of "clearing a path" so that the puppies will be able to find their source of nourishment. As parturition draws near, the breasts will have swelled with milk and the nipples will have enlarged and darkened to a rosy pink. If the hair in the breast region does not shed for some reason, you can easily cut it short with a pair of scissors or comb it out so that it does not mat and become a hindrance to the suckling pups later on.

PREPARING FOR THE PUPPIES

Prepare a whelping box a few days before the puppies are due, and allow the mother to sleep there overnight or to spend some time in it during the day to become accustomed to it. This way she is less likely to try to have her pups under the front porch or in the middle of your bed. A variety of places will serve, such as the corner of your cellar or garage (provided these places are warm and dry). An unused room, such as a dimly lit spare bedroom, can also serve as the place for delivery. If the weather is warm, a large outdoor dog house will do, as long as it is well protected from rain, drafts, and the cold—and enclosed by fencing or a run. A whelping box serves to separate mother and puppies from visitors and other distractions. The walls should be high enough to restrain the puppies yet low enough to allow the mother to take a short respite from her brood after she has fed them. Four feet square is minimum size (for most dogs) and six-to-eight-inch high walls will keep the pups in until they begin to climb; then side walls should be built up so that the young ones cannot wander away from their nest. As the puppies grow, they really need more room anyway, so double the space with a very low partition down the middle of the box, and soon you will find them naturally housebreaking themselves. Puppies rarely relieve themselves where they sleep. Layers of newspapers spread over the whole area will make excellent bedding and be absorbent enough to keep the surface warm and dry. These should be removed daily and replaced with another thick layer. An old quilt or washable blanket makes better footing for the nursing puppies than slippery newspaper during the first week; this is also softer for the mother to lie on.

Be prepared for the actual whelping several days in

advance. Usually the mother will tear up papers, refuse food, and become restless. These may be false alarms; the real test is her temperature, which will drop to below 100°F (38°C) about twelve hours before whelping. Take her temperature with a rectal thermometer, morning and evening, and usher her to her whelping box when her temperature goes down. Keep a close watch on her and make sure she stays safely indoors (or outdoors in a safe enclosure); if she is let outside, unleashed, or allowed to roam freely, she could wander off and start to go into labor. It is possible that she could whelp anywhere, and this could be unfortunate if she needs your assistance.

WHELPING

Usually little help is needed from you, but it is wise to stay close to be sure that the mother's lack of experience (if this is her first time) does not cause an unnecessary complication. Be ready to help when the first puppy arrives, for it could smother if she does not break the amniotic membrane enclosing it. She should tear open the sac and start licking the puppy, drying and stimulating it. Check to see that all fluids have been cleared from the pup's nostrils and mouth after the mother has licked her youngster clean; otherwise the pup may

have difficulty breathing. If the mother fails to tear open the sac and stimulate the newborn's breathing, you can do this yourself by tearing the sack with your hands and then gently rubbing the infant with a soft, rough towel. The afterbirth attached to the puppy by the long umbilical cord should follow the birth of each puppy. Watch to be sure that each afterbirth is expelled, for the retention of this material can cause infection. In her instinct for cleanliness the mother will probably eat the afterbirth after severing the umbilical cord. One or two meals of this will not hurt her; they stimulate her milk supply, as well as labor, for remaining pups. However, eating too many afterbirths can make her lose appetite for the food she needs to feed her pups and regain her strength. So remove the rest of them, along with the wet newspapers, and keep the box dry and clean.

If the mother does not bite the cord or bites it too close to the puppy's body, take over the job to prevent an umbilical hernia. Tearing is recommended, but you can cut the cord, about two inches from the body, with a sawing motion with scissors that have been sterilized in alcohol. Then dip the end of the cut cord in a shallow dish of iodine; the cord will dry up and fall off in a few days.

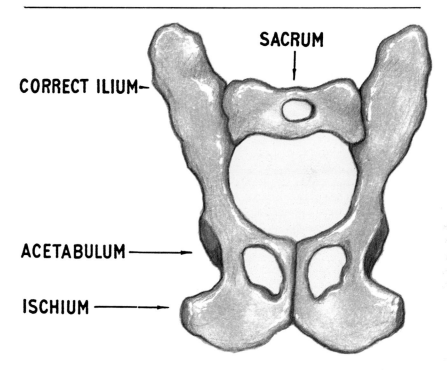

SACRUM

CORRECT ILIUM

ACETABULUM

ISCHIUM

Shape of pelvic entrance in the average female dog, showing adequate aperture through which the whelps have to pass.

The puppies should follow each other at intervals of not more than half an hour. If more time goes past and you are sure there are still pups to come, taking the mother for a brisk walk outside may start labor again. If she is actively straining without producing a puppy, the youngster may be presented backward, a so-called "breech" birth. Careful assistance with a well-lubricated finger to feel for the puppy or to ease it back may help, but never attempt to pull it out by force. This could cause serious damage, so seek the services of an expert—your veterinarian or an experienced breeder.

Even the best planned breeding can bear unexpected problems and complications. Therefore, do not rely solely on textbook knowledge of breeding and genetics. Experienced breeders and veterinarians will generally lend their words of wisdom—take full advantage of their generosity. Mere trial and error is no basis for any responsible breeding program.

If *anything* seems wrong during labor or parturition, waste no time in calling your veterinarian, who will examine the bitch and, if necessary, give her hormones to stimulate the birth of the remaining puppies. You may want his experience in whelping the litter even if all goes well. He will probably prefer to have the puppies born at his hospital rather than getting up in the middle of the night to come

A puppy nurser kit is considered standard equipment by many breeders. These kits are available at your local pet shop.

to your home. The mother would, no doubt, prefer to stay at home; but you can be sure she will get the best of care in a veterinary hospital. If the puppies are born at home, and all goes as it should, watch the mother carefully afterward. Within a day or two of the birth, it is wise to have the veterinarian check her and the pups to ensure that all is well.

Be sure each puppy finds a teat and starts nursing right away, as these first few meals supply colostral antibodies to help him fight disease. As soon as he is dry, hold each puppy to a nipple for a good meal without competition. Then he may join his littermates in the whelping box, out of his mother's way while she continues giving birth. Keep a supply of puppy formula on hand for emergency feedings or later weaning. An alternative formula of evaporated milk, corn syrup, and a little water with egg yolk can be warmed and fed if necessary. A pet nurser kit is also a good thing to have on hand; these are available at local pet shops. A supplementary feeding often helps weak pups (those that may have difficulty nursing) over the hump. Keep track of birth weights and weekly readings thereafter; this will furnish an accurate record of the pups' growth and health, and the information will be valuable to your veterinarian.

RAISING THE PUPPIES

After all the puppies have been born, take the mother outside for a walk and drink of water, and then return her to take care of her brood. She will probably not want to stay away for more than a minute or two for the first few weeks. Be sure to keep water available at all times and feed her milk or broth frequently, as she needs nourishment to produce milk. Encourage her to eat, with her favorite foods, until she seeks them of her own accord. She will soon develop a ravenous appetite and should have at least two large meals a day, with dry food available in addition. Your veterinarian can guide you on the finer points of nutrition as they apply to nursing dams.

Prepare a warm place to put the puppies after they are born to keep them dry and to help them to a good start in life. An electric heating pad, heat lamp or hot water bottle covered with flannel can be placed in the bottom of a cardboard box and near the mother so that she can see her puppies. She will usually allow you to help her care for the youngsters, but don't take them out of her sight. Let her handle things if your interference seems to make her nervous.

Be sure that all the puppies are getting enough to eat. If the mother sits or stands instead of lying still to nurse, the probable cause is scratching from the puppies' nails. You can remedy this by clipping them, as you would the bitch's, with a pet nail clipper. Manicure scissors also do for these tiny claws. Some breeders advise disposing of the smaller or weaker pups in a large litter, as the mother has trouble handling more than six or seven. You can help her out by preparing an extra puppy box or basket furnished with a heating pad and/or heating lamp and some bedding material. Leave half the litter with the mother and the other half in the extra box, changing off at two-hour intervals at first. Later you may exchange them less frequently, leaving them all together except during the day. Try supplementary feedings, too. As soon as their eyes open, at about two weeks, they will lap from a small dish.

WEANING THE PUPPIES

Normally the puppies should be completely weaned at five weeks, although you can start to feed them at three weeks. They will find it easier to lap semi-solid food than to drink milk at first, so mix baby cereal with whole or evaporated milk, warmed to body temperature, and offer it to the puppies in a saucer. Until they learn to lap it, it is best to feed one or two at a time because they are more likely to walk into it than to eat it. Hold the saucer at their chin level, and let them gather around, keeping paws off

Excessively long puppy nails can scratch the whelping mother's tummy and teats, making the bitch little inclined to nurse the pups. Specially designed clippers for trimming the nails are available at your local pet shop.

the dish. Cleaning with a damp sponge afterward prevents most of the cereal from sticking to the pups if the mother doesn't clean them up. Once they have gotten the idea, broth or babies' meat soup may be alternated with milk, and you can start them on finely chopped meat. At about four weeks, they will eat four meals a day and soon do without their mother entirely. Start them on canned dog food, or leave dry puppy food with them in a dish for self-feeding. Don't leave the water dish with them all the time; at this age everything is a play toy and they will use it as a wading pool. They can drink all they need if it is offered several times a day, after meals. As the puppies grow up, the mother will go into their "pen" only to nurse them, first sitting up and then standing. To dry up her milk supply completely, keep the mother away for longer periods; after a few days of part-time nursing she can stay away for even longer periods, and then permanently. The little milk left will be resorbed by her body.

The puppies may be put outside during the day, unless it is too cold or rainy, as soon as their eyes are open. They will benefit from the sunlight. A rubber mat or newspapers underneath will protect them from cold or dampness. As they mature, the pups can be let out for longer intervals, although you must provide them with a shelter at night or in bad weather. By now, cleaning up after the matured youngsters is a man-sized job, so put them out at least during the day and make your task easier. If you enclose them in a run or kennel, remember to clean it *daily*, as various parasites and other infectious organisms may be lurking if the quarters are kept dirty.

You can expect the pups to need at least one worming before they are ready to go to new homes. Before the pups are three weeks old, take a stool sample from each to your veterinarian. The vet can determine, by analyzing the stool, if any of the pups have worms—and if so, what kind of worms are present. If one puppy is infected, then all should be wormed as a preventive measure. Follow the veterinarian's advice; this also applies to vaccinations. You will want to vaccinate the pups at the earliest possible age. This way, the pups destined for new homes will be protected against some of the more debilitating canine diseases.

THE DECISION TO SPAY OR NEUTER

If you decide not to use your male or female for breeding, or if you are obligated to have the animal altered based on an agreement made between you and the seller, make the necessary arrangements with your veterinarian as soon as possible. The surgery involved for both males and females is relatively simple and painless: males will be castrated and females will have their ovaries and uterus removed. In both cases, the operation does not alter their personalities; you will, however, notice that males will be less likely to roam, to get into fights with other male dogs, and to mount objects and people.

Your veterinarian can best determine at what age neutering or spaying should be done. With a young female dog, the operation may be somewhat more involved, and as a result be more costly; however, in the long run you will be glad you made the decision to have this done for your pet. After a night or two at the veterinarian's or an animal hospital, your bitch can be safely returned to your home. Her stitches will heal in a short time, and when they are removed, you will hardly notice her souvenir scar of the routine operation. Once she has been spayed, she no longer will be capable of having a litter of puppies. Pet adoption agencies and other animal welfare organizations can house only so many animals at one time, given the money, space, and other resources they have available. This is why pet owners are urged to have their pets altered, so that puppies resulting from accidental breedings won't end up being put to sleep as so many others have that are lost, stray, unwanted, or abandoned.

Top view of a dog's skeletal structure. The dog is a highly specialized animal.

Dogs and the Law

BY ANMARIE BARRIE

No matter where you live, there will be laws and ordinances restricting the ownership of pets—exotic and wild animals (such as monkeys, pythons, and ocelots) as well as the more traditionally kept domestics (such as dogs and cats). This chapter purports to investigate with brevity the laws which pertain to the ownership and keeping of the domestic canine. Like all other things, laws change and evolve over time, and vary from locale to locale. The information supplied in this chapter is meant as a general guideline for the dog owner. Every owner is strongly encouraged to contact his local authorities to keep abreast on new laws and amendments to existing laws so that he can be the most responsible owner possible.

BUYING AND SELLING

Certain specific laws apply to the purchasing and peddling of pooches. Laws in these areas grow ever more stringent, so the potential buyer and/or seller is well advised to be aware of the laws pertaining to his transactions where dogs are concerned. Dealers and breeders, in most instances, are treated differently from the average dog owner who is trying to sell his first litter. Regardless, a sales contract is in order, a written agreement outlining the various dimensions of the sale. Sales contracts may indicate the quality of the dog, i.e.,

the pet-quality, show-quality, breeder-quality; the sex of the dog; and the breed of the dog. In addition to these basic essentials, the specifics, as registered with the national kennel club, should be included, i.e., the names and registration numbers of the sire and dam; the litter registration number; addresses of all involved, etc. Warranties and conditions of the sale should also be expressly stated, and no implications or unexpressed conditions may apply. For instance, the return policy, the guaranteed pedigree of the dog, the health of the dog (including the possibility of congenital defects in later years) should all be addressed. Replacement warranties are also appropriate to include, should something happen to the purchased puppy. Should a given puppy (of intended show-quality) begin to exhibit faults disqualified in the breed standard, the buyer is able to return the dog. Commonly, if the seller is no longer in the business of selling dogs, the buyer is entitled to half of the agreed-upon price.

GENERAL GUIDELINES FOR DOG OWNERS

"Give to God what is God's, give to Caesar what is Caesar's" is a Gospel quote that has been used and manipulated since it was originally uttered two thousand years ago. The concept of paying taxes has never sat well with humans, nor does it sit well with dogs. Licenses are basically taxes on dogs, though as pet owners we need not stew over the unfairness of "yet another tax." The purpose of licensing dogs is a valid and important one. Licenses serve as a positive means of identifying an animal and afford an owner with a fair chance of regaining his dog if lost or stolen. Licenses also provide a dog additional consideration by authorities and even from strangers, who will respect the fact the owner of this dog cares enough to identify it and affix its ID to its collar.

Many owners resist the call to license their dogs on the premise that their dogs are house dogs or yard dogs, or never ever walk off their leashes. Nonetheless, accidents and mishaps occur regularly, and it's better to be safe than sorry (why not be safe and law-abiding!?). The threat of impoundment and the treatment which dogs receive as a matter of course from such authorities should be scare tactic enough to persuade an owner to license his dog.

The cost of licenses varies from place to place as well as from dog to dog. Licenses for assistance dogs, such as Seeing Eye dogs, hearing dogs, or any handicap-assistance dogs, may be substan-

Dogs and the Law

tially less than a regular dog. In some areas, assistance dogs receive their licenses gratis, or are covered by their training agency. Recognizing the growing problem of dog over-population, many towns and cities offer reduced license fees for spayed and neutered dogs.

Vaccinations for dogs deserve special mention. Depending on where you live, the vaccination for rabies may or may not be mandatory. In some places, this vaccination is optional. While the chances of your well-kept canine acquiring rabies today may be minuscule, the cases are not so isolated and unheard of that an owner can rest in ultimate confidence. Generally a vaccinated dog can avoid being quarantined in the unfortunate event that it should bite a stranger or would-be assailant. The age for vaccination varies, but most usual is six months old. If a puppy is under the age of six months, it is advisable not to permit it to socialize with unknown dogs on the street. Keep in mind that vaccinations need to be kept updated for both rabies and other diseases.

Among the most common-sense concerns of current-day owners are leash laws. Responsible dog owners marvel with dismay over dogs which run the neighborhood without a collar, supervision, or their owner's concern. Caring dog proprietors are grateful for leash laws as it is the protection of the dog, as well as human passers-by, that is concerned. That a dog is under control at all times remains the premise of leash laws. Dogs that are given the "freedom" to wander the neighborhood or city block are likewise given the "right" to be impounded, snatched and/or injured. Fines are often issued against owners who do not abide by the leash laws of their community.

Running hand in hand, or paw in paw, with leash laws are muzzle ordinances. These laws require that a dog be muzzled at all times when it is in public. Although these laws are less commonplace than leash laws, they do exist in certain communities. Owners are advised to investigate if muzzle laws apply in their area.

Pooper-scooper laws are being enforced in more and more areas these days. "Curb Your Dog" signs have become as common as pedestrian crossings and "Yield signs." For the cleanliness of our communities, these kinds of laws are invented; in order to do our part as responsible dog owners and citizens, we must abide by these clean-up rules. While persons who live in the country have more gripes with these laws, city dwellers fully understand the need to observe these ordinances. Scoops are sold in pet shops, or you can employ simple plastic bags. It is assured that if you are the person walking behind the behind of a 250-pound pooch, you will be grateful for these laws. Some owners use brown paper sheets or newspapers (preferably yesterday's) to assist in the clean-up.

Anti-cruelty laws are geared towards the protection of animals on the whole, sparing dogs from potential, often unintentional, abuse. Laws such as these are sweeping the nations, as an increasing number of people become aware of deleterious situations arising for all animals. While active cruelty to an animal

evokes rage in any human being, there are more subtle displays of cruelty which these laws attempt to pinpoint—cruelty in the form of neglect and careless treatment. Persons who are found in violation of anti-cruelty laws are very often subject to fines. All citizens are encouraged to report any cases of cruelty which they witness or suspect to be happening. Commonly, ordinances prohibit the keeping of a dog in a parked car, which can be a cruel, irresponsible practice in most situations. Dogs have been known to suffer from heat prostration, and worse.

Anti-cruelty laws have also seeped into the world of puppy mills, as more and more of these

Dogs and the Law

unethical outfits are being undermined by concerned owners. The cruel treatment of animals in these farms must be combated by increased legislation. Always know the source of your potential new dog. Avoid sellers who cannot give you all the answers you want to know.

As heart-breaking and unimaginable as it seems, our dogs are not permitted in a great number of places. "No Dog" signs are frequently posted in buildings, parks, restaurants, motels, etc. It seems that dogs are more accepted in Continental countries, where dogs are permitted (even invited) to dine with the family at a fine restaurant. This not being the case in every American state or city of Great Britain, law-abiding citizens must contend with these restrictions.

Ordinances involving the number of dogs which an owner can keep are prevalent in most communities. These laws vary from place to place and from residency to residency. Whether you live in an apartment, condominium, house, or farm, there may be laws regulating the number of pets you are able to keep. Homes that wish to keep more than the maximum number of animals may be forced to apply for a kennel license or be subject to a daily fine and regular inspection.

For sake of neighbors and the general health of your family, it is wise to take these restrictions to heart. No matter how great your love of animals is, it is not humane to the animals involved to subject them to over-crowding and minimal attention. A small suburban apartment can quickly become the haven of 75 stray dogs and cats, should the owner so choose. Laws such as these prohibit these kinds of communes from blossoming all over the nation.

In most well-organized communities, there are organizations that specialize in Lost and Found dogs. For your dog's safety, you must have the dog licensed and vaccinated, as dogs that are protected in this way have a greater chance of finding their way back home, unscathed. If you have lost your dog, do not panic, but do work fast. The more people to whom you speak and angles that you take, the greater your chances of retrieving your lost pet. All local authorities (police, fire company, animal control organizations) and all types of media organizations (radio, newspapers, town crier) should be commissioned to lend a hand, keep out a keen eye and ear for the lost dog. Advertising through posters, newspapers, radio, and community lists will pay off in the end. Written descriptions, accompanied by photographs, can assist in helping people have a better mental image of the dog.

Prevention can never be overstressed. Licensing is a must, and the dog must wear the ID tag. Tattoos are quick becoming very popular. These should be located on the dog's inner thigh, not on its ear, as that appendage can easily be torn off by a thief. Tattoos have

Dogs and the Law

worked for generations on pack dogs, and the same philosophy of identification can work for pet owners too. Often, the dog's kennel club number or other identifying number is tattooed onto the dog.

Impoundment threatens lost dogs and all other dogs running at large, particularly those without collars and licenses. Most animal control authorities maintain the right to impound, sell, and/or destroy any animal that they catch. As an owner's legal property, a dog cannot be impounded or confiscated without the owner's notice. Of course, if the dog is loose and unidentified, the owner is knowingly waiving his rights, and thereby his chances of seeing that the dog has a fair chance to find its way home. A dog that proves itself a nuisance or dangerous to property and people may be confiscated; the owner may be notified ex post facto. An owner may then be invited to court to defend its dog's right to life.

Pounds, as a rule, are required

to keep a dog for a certain period of time before disposing of it in any permanent way. However, this period rarely exceeds four days in length, so owners must act expediently. The fortunate owner who does find his dog at the pound must have the dog vaccinated and licensed (if not done previously), as well as pay a fine. Unclaimed pets are either destroyed humanely or offered for adoption. Many pounds reserve the right to have the owner spay or neuter his unchained canine.

There are also laws that regard the disposal of a dog's remains. Owners must be aware of restrictions in this area. Under certain legislative bodies, a person is not allowed to bury his dog on his own property. In most cases, contacting your family veterinarian or a humane society to handle the details of burial is the most expeditious approach.

DOGS AS PROPERTY

Let there be no doubt about it: a dog is the personal property of its owner. This fact is well substantiated in the various legal codes and statutes under which we all live our daily lives. For dog owners, the dog's legal-property status can be considered a mixed blessing. On the one hand, the dog's legal status as property necessarily guarantees the owner certain rights under the law, the very same rights which pertain to the possession of other property. Homeowners especially should be familiar with some of these rights. On the other hand, the dog's status as legal property places very considerable responsibility on the shoulders of the dog owner, for he will be held legally accountable for the actions of his dog—

just as the homeowner is legally responsible for any injuries that occur on his property and are the result of, for example, negligence resulting from the owner's maintenance of the property.

For the dog owner to be entitled to the rights of a property owner pertinent to his dog, the dog in question must be licensed by the appropriate authorities, usually the local governing body. However, because of the nature of legal systems in most of the free countries, laws may vary from town to town, county to county, and state to state. Thus the owner is strongly encouraged to investigate the necessary requirements

for licensing his dog. At the same time, the owner is encouraged to ascertain the exact nature of the rights of a dog owner under the given laws applicable to the given place of residence.

This varying nature of laws makes it impossible for one to offer details on many of the rights and responsibilities of the dog owner. However, regardless of the place of residence, the dog owner is entitled to due process with regard to the taking of the licensed dog. Due process in this regard refers essentially to the necessary notification of the owner before any further action can be taken by the authorities. In this way, the owner is offered a chance to act on the behalf of his dog, his legal property.

An additional consequence of the legal-property status of the dog is that, as property, the dog cannot be considered a person under the law. One effect of this fact is that the dog therefore cannot be the beneficiary of a will; however, provisions for the care and continued maintenance of the dog can be, and should be, carefully spelled out in the will— just as it would be for the home or any other piece of property.

In summary, the dog is definitely considered property under the law. As such, the dog owner is entitled to given rights and held accountable for given responsibilities. To be granted these rights, the dog owner must license his dog, as well as follow any other guidelines required under the laws of his or her place of residence. Finally, as property, the dog cannot be considered a person, and this fact holds various implications.

Because the dog is the legal property of the dog owner, the dog owner is legally responsible for the behavior of his dog, as well as for the care and maintenance of the animal. However, when the dog is in the possession of a person other than the owner, such as a temporary caretaker, that other person may be held responsible for the dog, depending on the specific circumstances involved

and the specific laws of the jurisdiction in which the action(s) occurs. To offer an example, consider the following scenario: A dog is owned by Mr. Smith, who leaves on vacation and hires an individual to care for his dog. While Mr. Smith is on vacation, the dog caretaker walks the dog without a leash and the dog bites a child. Of course, because the dog is property and not person, someone must be held accountable. Should it be Mr. Smith or the caretaker? In such a case it is likely that the caretaker would be held accountable for the dog's biting of the child, provided of course that Mr. Smith did not leave directions to walk the dog without a leash, etc. As we can

Dogs and the Law

see, many variables can come into play regarding legal responsibility for the dog.

To keep it simple in an attempt to offer the reader as much information as possible without getting weighed down in extraneous details, a few general guidelines will be presented.

First, the dog owner, for all intents and purposes, should raise, train, and keep his dog under the assumption that he is legally responsible for every action and for the entire well-being of his dog, ranging from obeying pooper-scooper laws to anti-cruelty laws to dog-bite statutes. In this way, the owner will act as

responsibly as possible and, in the end, avoid possible law suits. Secondly, whenever leaving the dog in the custody of others, whether for a short time or a prolonged period, the dog owner should leave clear, explicit written directions regarding proper and appropriate care of the dog. These directions can be prepared ahead of time and kept on file by the owner for use whenever the need arises. In so doing, the owner protects himself in the case of a lawsuit. Thirdly, a minor can be held legally responsible for the dog as property, and this fact needs to be considered whenever a youngster is in charge of the dog. Lastly, the dog owner must familiarize himself with the laws that pertain to him as a dog owner, as a resident of his given community. In no other way can the dog owner act responsibly and thus be protected under the law.

Because the dog owner is legally responsible for his dog, he is liable for all damages and personal injuries that result from the dog. Under strict liability, the owner is liable for any damages or injury caused by the dog, even if they are not the "fault" of the owner. Of course, common law doctrines are the products of court decisions, and thus may vary from place to place. Additionally,

liability may be subject to the same circumstantial variables as those which apply to responsibility in general.

Because the owner is liable for the actions of his dog, he can be taken to court and sued. A person injured by a dog will likely receive reimbursement for all medical expenses, as well as a given sum for pain and suffering, depending on the circumstances. The same conditions apply to damages: a person can receive full reimbursement for the loss or damage of any property that was the product of the dog's actions. In serious cases, e.g., those involving blatant negligence, malice or forethought,

Dogs and the Law

the owner of the dog can be sentenced to prison and/or fined.

The subject of vicious dogs abounds in controversy, in part because of the lack of an all-encompassing definition of viciousness as it pertains to the dog and in part because there is a current trend to label entire breeds of dog as inherently vicious. Because of the controversial nature of the vicious-dog subject, the reader is encouraged to do two things: first, read up on the specific laws pertaining to canine viciousness that apply to his locale; and second, to employ utmost common sense in the execution of his dog-owning responsibilities. The first step is by far the easier of the two, for vicious-dog statutes can be found in most libraries and at many municipal buildings. Beginning with inquiries and following up with research ensures the dog owner expedient acquisition of the applicable laws regarding viciousness and his dog. The second step, regarding the application of common sense to all aspects of canine ownership, requires that the dog owner first obey all laws pertinent to his ownership, e.g., leash laws, proper training, housing, restriction, etc.; second be well aware and understand the nature of his charge and adjust its keeping accordingly; and lastly take all steps necessary to ensure that others who may care for the dog be explicitly instructed on how to execute their caretaker task.

By following the two-step process just described to help you guard against a potential vicious-dog law suit, especially in following the application of common sense to your dog ownership, you to a large degree also work to prevent injury, both to yourself and to others. In so doing, you are also necessarily limiting the possibility that you will find yourself beside your dog in court over your dog's injuring another person.

To assist the dog owner in applying common sense to his dog ownership, the following principles are presented: (1) all dogs, meaning each and every dog, no matter how small or large a dog, young or old a dog, has the potential to injure a person; (2) dogs act largely on instinct and perceive the world much differently than people do, i.e., a dog may see a situation as dangerous and react with fear biting even though a person sees the situation as perfectly non-threatening or even pleasant; (3) not all people are dog fanciers, and some people even delight in provoking and taunting an animal, which can easily lead to their being injured; (4) dogs do not treat all people in the same manner as they treat you, their owner and caretaker.

By considering these principles, obeying the laws of dog ownership (which essentially are designed for the protection of you, your dog, and others), and consistently applying common sense in your daily doggie doings, you by and large prevent injury.

In recent years, insurance companies have offered insurance policies to dog owners. Essentially these policies can be grouped into two general categories: canine life insurance and liability insurance. Of course, many different policies from each category are offered, and the cost of the respective policy varies roughly in accordance with the coverage offered. For example, a "life" insurance policy that covered accidental injury as well as providing a death benefit will typically cost more

than a policy that offers only a death benefit, provided of course that the death benefits are of equivalent value.

Canine insurance is not for every dog owner, though every dog owner is encouraged to investigate the various policies offered and for themselves make the determination of whether yea or nay they purchase such insurance. Common consensus offers that canine insurance is best suited for two kinds of dog owners, a splitting that roughly corresponds to the two kinds of canine insurance offered. The first kind of owner is the professional breeder and/or showperson, who has invested large sums of money in his individual dogs and stands to lose much in the case of accidental injury or death. Such a person is strongly encouraged to investigate the canine life insurance available. In short, he is encouraged to protect his investment.

The second type of person is the owner of a guard dog or any dog trained or demonstrating the proclivity to attack a person. For this dog owner, investigation of some type of liability insurance is encouraged.

After all is said and done, after all steps and measures towards responsible lawful ownership have been taken, there may still come a time when the dog owner finds himself in the midst of a controversy. The cause may be a very simple or insignificant one, or it may be a very complex one. The important point to remember is that a controversy must be managed in a legal and responsible way.

If the controversy is a minor one, it might be best to attempt to resolve the the problem between the two parties, in which case a third party (an objective mediator) often proves helpful. If this fails for any reason, e.g., tempers, then going to the authorities is strongly recommended. In no case should anyone attempt to take matters into their own hands, becoming judge, jury, and executioner all in one. If the controversy involves a serious matter, you are encouraged to seek legal advice as soon as possible. Remember that you are responsible for the actions of your dog, and therefore you can be held liable for any damages or injuries that your dog may inflict. All controversies should be approached in an objective manner; the dog owner must realize that there are at least two sides to the story and that resolution of the conflict will likely involve at least small compromises from each of the parties involved.

CRUELTY

What determines or defines cruelty to animals often excites great controversy in our society.

Anti-cruelty legislation, nonetheless, continues to make headway, as new laws are being enforced with regularity. Avoiding the inhumane treatment of animals, neglect and abuse should be the target of all caring dog owners. The conditions of a breeding facility or animal shelter, cosmetic alterations of puppies (cropping ears and docking tails), protocol for dealing with an injured animal, and impoundment of lost, vicious or destructive dogs are just some of the topics which anti-cruelty laws address. In the United States, ear cropping and tail docking are not prohibited as they are in Great Britain. Britain has for generations deemed such cosmetic alterations unnecessary and unnecessarily cruel.

Air travel can be a more difficult matter. Airlines most usually allow dogs to fly on their flights. Small dogs can be carried on, while large ones need to be kept in the baggage area. Of course the appropriate crate is required for any dog traveling by air. Mark the crate: "Live Cargo" or "This End Up" for the safety of your canine luggage. Travel agents are usually well informed and will advise you on such decisions.

LANDLORDS AND DOGS

Regardless of how it may seem, there is no *natural* antipathy between landlords and dogs. Dogs in themselves are no more the natural enemy of landlords

TRAVEL

When traveling with your dog, there are a number of considerations with which to be concerned. The most common method of travel is automobiles, though fewer laws address this mode of transportation. Regarding urban travel, i.e., buses, subways, rails, dogs are usually not permitted on board unless the dog is an assistance dog. Some railways allow dogs to stay in the owner's cabin, while others require that the dog be kept in the baggage compartment (likely there is an area especially equipped for live cargo). Always check with the railway and train station about the regulations regarding your dog. Do this before leaving home! If you intend to travel by sea, less common in today's world of airplanes, it is advised that similar inquiries be made to the ship's station.

than, say, tenants are. Landlords and dogs don't get along for the most part because in many cases dogs and tenants—both dog owners and non-dog owners—don't get along. Landlords often try to outlaw the ownership of dogs by their tenants simply because dogs make trouble. They can be destructive, they can make messes, they can scare people, they can hurt people. To avoid the trouble that dogs can make, landlords write into their leases clauses that prohibit the keeping of dogs by tenants. Landlords in general might not be the nicest people in the world, but you can't blame them for wanting to avoid trouble and expense that tenants' pet dogs may bring them. For

example, would you as landlord relish the idea of being sued by some troublemaking yardbird who, while visiting one of your tenants, was bitten by his homicidal cur? And don't ask why he'd be suing the landlord when it wasn't the landlord's dog that bit him—he'd be suing everyone in sight, as the courts encourage that type of madness: wouldn't a reasonably prudent landlord provide 24-hour guard service to make sure that visitors are not attacked in their buildings?

Governmental units at various levels are telling landlords that they can't tell their tenants not to own dogs (or cats), and various courts are starting to tell landlords that either their leases don't say what they plainly do say or that they say it but the courts don't like it and will therefore come up with a reason why it shouldn't be allowed. But the milennium for dog-owning apartment dwellers has not yet arrived; until it does, the best thing a tenant can do is to ask for permission from the owner...and to get it in writing.

Index